Media Portrayals
of Terrorism

Robert G. Picard

Media Portrayals of Terrorism

FUNCTIONS AND MEANING OF NEWS COVERAGE

 IOWA STATE UNIVERSITY PRESS / AMES

For Anna Elisabeth

Robert G. Picard, a professor at California State University, Fullerton, was project director of the Terrorism and the News Media Research Project for the Association for Education in Journalism and Mass Communication, Mass Communications and Society Division.

© 1993   Iowa State University Press, Ames, Iowa 50010
All rights reserved
Manufactured in the United States of America
⊗ This book is printed on acid-free paper.

First edition, 1993

Library of Congress Cataloging-in-Publication Data

Picard, Robert G.
    Media portrayals of terrorism : functions and meaning of news coverage / Robert G. Picard.—
1st ed.
        p.   cm.
    Includes bibliographical references and index.
    ISBN 0-8138-1842-7
    1. Terrorism in the press. 2. Terrorism and mass media. 3. Terrorism—Political aspects.
4. Press and politics—20th century. 5. Press—Objectivity—20th century. 6. Terrorism and
mass media—20th century. I. Title.
PN4784.T45P5   1993
303.6′25—dc20   90-20959

Contents

Crimes will always remain crimes and terror will always remain terror, even if carried out in the name of higher principles . . . or to defend oneself against something that appears even more abominable.

Olof Palme

Preface

TERRORISM GENERATES intrinsically emotional responses. During the past decade, the American public became well aware of acts of terrorism because of media coverage of these acts of violence and because political leaders made the phenomena a major issue.

By the mid-1980s, the growing salience of the issue and a general lack of detached consideration about terrorism led me and other scholars to begin significant consideration of the role of media in conveying information about terrorism, of the functions of that coverage, and of the inherent meaning attached to information about terrorism and terrorists. Our concerns included not only the role of media coverage but also the type of coverage that occurred and its effects.

Although political figures and political scientists had boldly asserted that media played a pathological role in terrorist events for more than a decade, little scholarship based on scientific knowledge of and social science literature concerning the roles and effects of propaganda and persuasion, media portrayals of violence, and interpretation of information existed in the literature. The lack of literature written from a communications perspective, with an understanding of communication theory and practice, was disturbing, especially given politicians' attacks against media coverage of terrorism and calls for censorship and other controls of information.

In addition, much of the coverage appeared to lack objectivity and to define terrorism by who committed acts of violence rather than what acts were committed. Thus, violent acts by groups opposed by political leaders or the media would be labeled terrorism and the perpetrators called terrorists, but similar acts by groups supported by political leaders or the media would not be so characterized.

In 1985, the Mass Communications and Society Division of the Association for Education in Journalism and Mass Communication organized the Terrorism and the News Media Research Project to help improve knowledge and understanding about the roles of media in terrorism, the nature of media coverage, and the effects of the coverage. Researchers from a variety of disciplines—including communications, political science, criminology, psychology, and sociology—were brought together to help promote inquiry, exchange information, and develop significant information on these topics. I was asked to serve as project director and administrator of that project.

After five years of study, nearly every member of that group has come to the conclusion that media do not cause terrorism, but they can make it worse by poor reporting practices, by allowing themselves to be manipulated by interested parties, and by not giving audiences a better understanding of the issue.

This book represents my understanding of media's role in terrorism, the functions played by media, and the meaning assigned to terrorism as a result of media coverage. It was written with the intent of drawing together what is known about media and terrorism to provide scholars of communications and political science, politicians, journalists, and other interested parties information about media-terrorism relationships. The opinions expressed in the book are my own and not necessarily those of other researchers or the Association for Education in Journalism and Mass Communication.

Many persons and organizations assisted and encouraged the project and my own scholarship. I cannot begin to thank them all, but I wish to acknowledge the encouragement and support offered by Yonah Alexander, Institute for the Study of International Terrorism, State University of New York; Ron Crelinsten, Department of Criminology, University of Ottawa; Brian Jenkins, Rand Corporation; Abe Miller, Department of Political Science, University of Cincinnati; Ralph Dowling, Department of Speech Communication, Ball State University; and Rick Stephens, College of Journalism, University of South Carolina.

Media Portrayals
of Terrorism

1

Introduction

● When members of the Shining Path group blew up a tourist bus in Lima in July 1989, injuring two dozen Soviet sailors, Peruvian authorities called it an act of terrorism.

● When Armenian nationalists attempted to assassinate the Turkish ambassador to Hungary in December 1991, in a continuation of the long-standing Armenian-Turkish territorial dispute, Turkish officials called the shooting terrorism.

● When Sikhs seeking an independent homeland opened fire from an automobile, killing twenty-three persons at a market and mill in Tohana, India, in December 1991, Indian authorities called the act terrorism.

● When Israeli military forces abducted Muslim cleric Sheik Abdel Karim Obeid from Lebanon in July 1989, Arab leaders and officials worldwide called the hostage taking an act of terrorism.

● When rebel military forces attacked Tbilisi in an effort to oust Georgian President Zviad Gamsakhurdia in December 1991, he called the rebellion terrorism.

● When members of the Ulster Freedom Fighters opened fire in a betting shop in a Catholic area of Belfast, Northern Ireland, killing five elderly patrons in February 1992, British authorities called the attack terrorism.

THESE INCIDENTS ILLUSTRATE different understandings and uses of the word *terrorism* to describe acts of violence and the problems of perspective and definition one encounters when discussing the issue. It has become an axiom that terrorism describes acts of violence committed by others and that similar violence committed by one's own nation, or by those with whom one sympathizes, is legitimate violence. The confusion

3

over the definition is understandable because misuse and disuse of the word are tools of political communication that help construct public images of those who use violence to achieve their goals.

This book explores the issue of terrorism by attempting to reduce the confusion about its definition, goals, and practice, and about the role of communication, particularly mass communication, in acts of violence. The definition of terrorism will be more fully explored in Chapter 2, but to begin this discussion, *terrorism* will be defined as violence or threat of violence, designed to induce fear, as a strategy for achieving some goal.

Acts of terrorism are thus symbolic acts designed to carry messages from the perpetrators of the violence to various audiences. Because terrorism is a form of communication, the means by which its message is disseminated, reported, and discussed are crucial. Media make it possible for the communication to be rapidly disseminated to wide audiences, and the media portrayals affect the meaning that is assigned to the events by the audiences.

In the majority of incidents, the most important element in communication about terrorist acts is not the acts themselves but the meaning assigned to the acts by media, authorities, and the populace. What is said about the acts and how the acts are interpreted play a greater role in determining the impact and significance of the acts than does the violence itself. L. John Martin has observed that "communication derives meaning from the whole gambit of human behavior so long as at least two individuals are interacting. Terrorism is a form of human behavior that is loaded with significance."[1] Because media play a significant role in conveying messages that help audiences assign that meaning, their role in the process is of particular interest.

The importance of these symbolic acts in sending messages has led Alex P. Schmid and Janny de Graaf to argue that the violence itself is a form of language and must be considered as a communicative act.

> In our view terrorism can best be understood as a violent communication strategy. There is a sender, the terrorist, a message generator, the victim, and a receiver, the enemy, and/or the public. The nature of the terrorist act, its atrocity, its location and the identity of its victim serve as generators for the power of the message. Violence, to become terroristic, requires witnesses.[2]

Although accepting terrorism as an act of communication, I reject the suggestion that such political violence takes place solely as an act of communication. Instead I see terrorism as a purposive strategy of warfare and social change that employs symbolic violence as a vehicle for communication to a variety of audiences as one of its tactics.

Messages conveyed through the symbolic acts of political violence can be fully interpreted, however, only when one understands to whom they are directed and how communication channels are used in the communication process. The intended receiver of messages varies in different terrorist acts. In various cases messages are being sent to governments, to the populace, to sponsors of terrorism, or even to other perpetrators of terrorism. The intended audience might be domestic, that is, in the nation in which the violence is located, or it might be located in a foreign nation. Awareness of the acts is needed for the acts to be effective. Awareness can be generated by a variety of means, one of which is media coverage. But even without the facilitation of mass media, terrorist acts can be effective if their messages reach their intended audience through personal or specialized media (such as telephone reports or daily reports of government security services) or other communication channels. Identification of the intended audience and the channels of communication that carry messages is key in understanding these symbolic acts and is crucial in understanding the role of media in carrying news about terrorism.

News coverage of terrorism has been criticized in recent decades, and that criticism is not without basis. There is probably no type of news event that presents more obstacles to coverage, is fraught with more pitfalls, or has the potential for greater manipulation of the media than incidents of terrorism. The criticism is based on several assumptions about terrorism and about its relationship to media: (1) that violence undertaken for social or political purposes is aberrant behavior rather than the norm, (2) that violence is perpetrated only by those on the fringes of or outside the boundaries of society, (3) that media coverage is an essential element for the existence of terrorism, (4) that terrorists seek publicity about their acts, (5) that media throughout the world cover terrorism using the same news values and definitions of news, (6) that media throughout the world cover terrorism as a means of fulfilling similar social functions, and (7) that perpetrators of political violence specifically play to U.S. and other Western news media.[3]

These assumptions serve as the presuppositions used by critics in constructing logical-appearing syllogistic arguments about the impact of news coverage. Those concerned about the impact of media on terrorism usually begin with these assumptions as their base. Just as there are problems with the way the word *terrorism* is commonly used, there are significant problems and contradictions within these assumptions. If one does not consider the validity of the assumptions, one quickly falls into a narrow area of discussion that excludes most acts of terrorism and leads to unsupported and fallacious conclusions.

Even a cursory examination of the first assumption quickly leads to its rejection. Acts of violence undertaken for social or political purposes are clearly the norm rather than the exception for the human species. The recorded history of mankind is dominated by violence committed against others by individuals, tribes, religious and ethnic groups, and nations pursuing their social or political goals through threat and violence. Writing on the problem of terrorism, Yonah Alexander notes:

> Terrorism, as an expedient tactical and strategic tool of politics in the struggle for power within and among nations, is not new in the history of man's inhumanity to man. From time immemorial opposition groups, functioning under varying degrees of stress, have intentionally utilized instruments of psychological and physical force—including intimidation, coercion, repression and, ultimately, destruction of lives and property—for the purpose of attaining real or imaginary ideological and political goals.[4]

Thus, considering social and political violence by mankind as aberrant behavior ignores reality. This is not to argue that such violence is acceptable, but that it is clearly within the normally encountered behavior of social relations.

The assumption that acts of terrorism come from outside society immediately limits discussion of terrorism to only those individuals and groups who have rejected the norms of, and their own positions in, a given society and to groups from other nations or societies who use terrorism to carry out their goals. This demarcation of terrorism as an outside threat makes it possible to ignore internal acts of terrorism committed by governments and their supporters or internal dissident groups that have not fully rejected the society. If one accepts this assumption, one removes from discussion of terrorism the largest proportion of violence, that undertaken by state terrorists (military and security forces committing terroristic acts with or without official orders or paramilitary groups supported by governments and carrying out such violence as government surrogates).

The third assumption, that media coverage is crucial to terrorism, is also false. Acts of terrorism existed thousands of years prior to the development of either print or broadcast communication, and they exist today in nations where the media are controlled by the various state apparatuses and incidents of terrorism either are not reported or are sparsely reported. Although the existence of media is not a necessary condition for terrorism, it can clearly be useful to those who perpetrate political violence and is thus an element worthy of consideration by those concerned about violence. But media must be considered modern tools of terrorists, just as are weapons and explosives and aircraft and ships.

A fourth assumption is that terrorists seek publicity for their acts. Although many terrorist groups are publicity seekers, there are also perpetrators of terrorism who avoid publicity and do not make claims of responsibility or engage in press relations to promote their activities and causes. This is the case for some insurgent terrorist groups and almost universally true of those who commit state terrorism.

Critics also link terrorism and media by making sweeping generalizations about the role of media worldwide, without accounting for significantly different approaches to the functions of media and the norms of media behavior throughout the world. Most criticism is based on Western media models and assumes that media in the remainder of the world operate similarly. This is clearly not the case; scholars of comparative media have revealed widely different purposes and operations of media.[5]

The sixth assumption, that media coverage worldwide serves similar social functions, is debatable. Coverage of terrorist acts in one country may serve to turn the population against the perpetrators, whereas coverage of the same acts in another country may serve to arouse passions to support and perpetrate similar acts.

The seventh assumption, that terrorists play to U.S. and Western media, is also debatable. Clearly, there are instances in which terrorists seek the audiences these media provide, but most terrorism is not international and is directed at domestic audiences in the nations where the violence takes place or at regional audiences in the nations surrounding the location of the act. Indeed, access to worldwide and Western media is severely limited in locations where much terrorism takes place, and efforts to reach the audiences of worldwide media or Western audiences account for only a small amount of terrorist actions.

If these seven assumptions are put aside, one can view the issue of social and political violence in a broader, less subjective form. From this vantage point, terroristic violence is not seen as unusual human behavior; it can be perpetrated from within or without a society by individuals, groups, and social institutions. Media can be used to increase exposure to and place meaning upon these symbolic acts of violence. Those analyzing the use of media and its impact must do so in terms of the particular social settings in which specific terrorist acts take place, with an understanding of the symbolic purposes of each act, the meaning assigned to an act by its perpetrators, the uses made of media, and the meaning assigned to the act by authorities, media, and audiences.

Terrorist violence undertaken by individuals who have completely rejected a society in which they were members and by individuals who never were part of the society under attack challenges the legitimacy and stability of the institutions of that society. When terrorism is perpetrated by individuals or groups that have chosen to stay within a society, these perpetrators most often seek to alter distributions of power or social norms in the society, or to repress those who wish to achieve social change. In either type of violence, the government and the media are forced into adversarial conflict well beyond that experienced in their normal, day-to-day relationship because the media do not always serve the interests of the government.

Terrorism, then, involves a complex nexus of three actors: (1) those who engage in violence to achieve political goals, (2) authorities reacting to such incidents, and (3) members of media organizations who might report on events of public importance and impact. A fourth element — the victims of violence and their families and friends — is clearly involved in incidents of terrorism; however, these people participate not as actors but rather as props used by the actors.

The news value of incidents of terrorism is not in question. Kidnappings, bombings, hijackings, assassinations, and the slaughter of civilians are by nature public acts deserving of coverage. What most concerns many critics about the role of news coverage of terrorism is that the immediacy of coverage and the event-centered nature of such reporting can play into the hands of those undertaking political violence. This is especially true in the case of terrorists who want coverage to help them achieve their purposes. Journalistic norms about event coverage have also made it possible for governments to use the media to explain and expose the attacks in ways that help authorities achieve their goals. The media themselves have been willing to manipulate both other actors, using the victims and the families of victims for their own purposes as well.

Media have been criticized for their tendency to ignore "average" terrorist acts, the small-scale violence that occurs daily, instead concentrating coverage on spectacular or large-scale acts of violence. Most coverage of terrorism is extraordinary coverage of extraordinary acts of terrorism. The frequent deaths of one or two persons in bombings or shootings are generally ignored by media outside the locality in which they occur. Media audiences therefore come to associate terrorism only with spectacular events perpetrated by disaffected persons.

Indeed, if one reviews criticism of press coverage of acts of terrorism in recent years, nearly all the concerns grow out of problems associated with coverage of fewer than a half a dozen incidents, including press handling of the Hanafi Muslim takeover of the B'nai B'rith headquarters in Washington, D.C., in 1977; the takeover of the U.S. embassy in Tehran in 1979; and the hijacking of TWA Flight 847 to Beirut in 1985. Coverage of these types of incidents has been criticized for sensationalism, narrowness, endangering lives and effective public policy, and interfering with government operations.

Other concerns about media coverage result from what many individuals, attempting to explain specific incidents of violence and to halt future violence, see as a contagion effect of news coverage.[6] These critics argue that coverage of acts of terrorism, especially large quantities of coverage, causes other groups to imitate the acts that gained coverage. Some have gone so far as to argue that if there were less coverage, particularly on television, spectacularly violent acts of hostage taking and attacks on civilians would disappear. Others argue that the agenda-setting and status-conferral effects of news coverage provide terrorists with the publicity and legitimacy they desire and that such coverage serves the terrorists' needs more than the needs of society. As a result, these critics contend that fewer groups would seek recognition through such political violence if coverage were limited.[7]

Media clearly have a responsibility for their coverage of political violence because the coverage can have, and has had, deleterious effects. Exploration of the effects of media coverage demonstrates that the media can spread hysteria, interfere with officials' efforts to cope with terrorism, and provide the attention, recognition, and legitimacy desired by those who commit such acts. Coverage also has been shown to have beneficial effects in helping the public and government understand and cope with terrorism and, possibly, in reducing the necessity for violence.

This book will explore the problems and benefits of media coverage of terrorist acts and analyze research that provides an understanding of the role of media in terrorism. It will examine the socio-institutional context of terrorism and communication, and terrorism as persuasion, and will then explore specific issues, problems, and criticisms of media coverage. Before discussion of those issues can be undertaken, it is necessary to define terrorism and to review the extent, nature, major perpetrators, and types of terrorist attacks, as well as how these attacks are interpreted by officials and scholars, so that the reader can have a better understanding of the milieu in which the relationship between media and terrorism must be analyzed.

2

Understanding
Terrorism

AS SYMBOLS, the words used to describe concepts can be employed in a variety of denotative and connotative ways that lead to a contamination of whatever purity of meaning the words had at their origin. The word *terrorism* has suffered considerable corruption because of the ways it has been employed by those who wish to describe political violence in a polemical fashion. Terrorism has been used in a wide variety of ways to denote everything from all antigovernment violence to all political violence.

The word *terrorism* has been used to describe the actions of small organizations with little support that reject existing society, large groups with wide popular support that oppose a particular regime, and governments that use violence to maintain or expand their power.[1] It has been used as a semantic weapon to place dissenters far outside the parameters of social norms, thus allowing societies to refuse to deal with the individuals and/or to act against "terrorists" in ways that would not be tolerated against "civilized" persons.

Terrorism, thus, has many definitions and meanings, few of which are well developed. The differences in definitions result from different viewpoints and interpretations of political violence. Legal, political, psychological, and moral approaches to this form of violence have brought widely differing definitions. Legal definitions emphasize criminal aspects of the acts and approach those acts as violations of national or international laws. Political definitions emphasize aspects related to government interests, including military and political characteristics and threats to governments and their allies. Psychological definitions of terrorism emphasize the cognitive aspects of the acts, especially their effects on the population. Moral definitions contain normative judgments about the acts, emphasizing social and religious norms and values against violence and the killing of humans. In recent years social scientists have attempted to develop detached definitions that do not overemphasize any one approach but, rather, attempt to encompass different facets from the various approaches represented here. This has been done to ameliorate the use of definitions as semantic tools for use against dissidents and as a means of ignoring the significant use of terror by governments. In addition, these definitions have attempted to reduce the associative aspects of biased definitions that evoke other negative associations and make meaningful discussions of the phenomenon difficult.

In these broader definitions, the most commonly included elements are (1) the use of violence or force, (2) the use of threat or intimidation, (3) the inducement of fear or terror in the population, and (4) the use of these elements as part of a purposive strategy for achieving goals.

This book embraces a broad definition that reduces the semantic difficulties and that uses the word *terrorism* in a neutral sense that applies to all who use its tactics of violence. In this book, terrorism will be understood as violence or threat of violence, in which civilians or locations habituated by civilians are targets or are frequently involved in the conflict. In its widest form, the term can be used to denote three major types of terrorist acts: pathological terrorism, criminal terrorism, and political/social terrorism (Figure 2.1).

Pathological terrorism is usually nonpolitical and often the work of mentally unbalanced individuals. It is rarely a group activity, but it can be as shown by the murders and assassination attempts of the so-called Manson family in the 1960s and 1970s.

Criminal terrorism is also nonpolitical, normally carried out for economic gain. It is sometimes perpetrated by individuals but is often the work of organized groups, such as the Mafia and Oriental triads or tongs. In such situations, protection rackets, extortion, and attacks on rivals and opponents are often involved. Recent examples of criminal terrorism include drug tampering in the United States, poisoning of candy in Japan as a means of extorting money from manufacturers, and killings of government officials and journalists in Colombia and other Latin American nations by drug trafficking cartels (a type of violence called *narco-terrorism* in the parlance of popular media).

Political/social terrorism includes ideologically based violence that

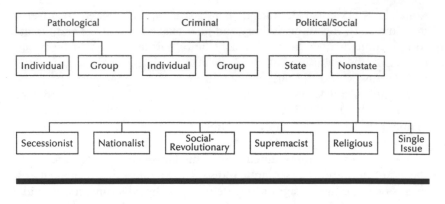

2.1 Typology of terrorism.

is part of an effort to attack social and political institutions. This, of course, is the kind of violence that most people think of when they think of terrorism, and it is a subcategory of the political/social terrorism called *nonstate terrorism.* Such violence is organized, planned action to achieve specific goals that can be political, religious, social, or economic in nature. This type of activity is nearly always carried out by groups rather than single individuals. When governments engage in terrorism or when they support groups that do so, they also fall into the broad political/social terrorism category in a subcategory called *state terrorism.*

Nonstate terrorism is further divided into classifications that reveal the great differences in purposes and motivations of terrorist groups. These classifications are secessionist, nationalist, social-revolutionary, supremacists (ethnic/racial supremacist organizations), religious, and single issue.

This book is concerned with the political/social violence category of terrorism and will use the word *terrorism* to mean that category and the word *terrorist* to refer to all who use the tactics of terrorism as described in the definition. Thus, the killing of Lord Mountbatten by the Irish nationalists is considered terrorism, as are attacks against agricultural cooperatives in Nicaragua by the so-called contras. Attacks on buses in Israel by Palestinian nationalists are classified as terrorism, as is the starvation of the population of Eritrea and Tigre caused by the Ethiopian government's halting food shipments to those rebel-held regions of the country.

Purposes of Terrorism

Although it is somewhat popular to characterize terrorism as the acts of lunatics, doing so is quite inaccurate. Important functions in the strategy of terrorists are served by the attacks, and such violence is rarely undertaken for the sake of the violence itself.

As purposive action, terrorism is undertaken by groups to achieve their goals. Individual acts of terrorism are rarely conceived as a means of achieving an overall goal or major military victory but are means by which limited objectives might be met. These include (1) revenge or retaliation for acts by the government or its supporters against the group, (2) attempts to liberate group members incarcerated by the government or its allies, (3) promotion of group morale and allegiance by proving the group's effectiveness, (4) acquisition of funds or supplies needed by the group, and (5) spreading fear. In the case of state terrorism, the purposes are generally to (1) repress dissent, (2) promote international policies, and (3) spread fear as a means of inhibiting internal and external opposition.

An important objective of many terrorist attacks is the creation of the *propaganda of the deed*, that is, the act itself carrying messages. Normally the messages are that the terrorists are effective, that they are to be taken seriously, that not all individuals in the society are happy with the status quo, and that the authorities are not in full control. Using violent acts against social institutions and civilian populaces to carry these messages makes it possible for terrorist groups to avoid direct violent confrontation with authorities—which would usually bring a quick end to the groups—and still to have messages conveyed to audiences through these incidents of violence.

A third purpose of terrorist acts is the spreading of uncertainty and fear among the population. When the populace becomes aware of the terrorist acts, the situation creates disorientation, anxiety, and fear for survival that terrorists can exploit. Although individual terrorist actions are not expected to be the coup de grace against an opponent, they can play an important part in a campaign toward that larger goal. By disorienting individuals and creating insecurity and the loss of confidence in officials, the acts can mobilize the population against the government and generate popular support needed to overthrow government or allow others to do so. In the case of state terrorism, the creation of fear is undertaken for the purpose of keeping the population from aiding dissidents or joining their causes.

Because nonstate terrorist acts challenge the legitimacy and stability of governments, achieving a reaction by government is often part of terrorists' strategy. If the reaction is unduly repressive, it will generate more instability and lead others to question the legitimacy of the government.

In some cases, perpetrators of terrorism are not attempting to topple a government but are using the acts of violence as a means of gaining social or political recognition of their views or of leading the government to acquiesce to their demands.

Terrorists also seek forums for their causes. Because media are an institution in society that supports and helps perpetuate the basic norms and values of the dominant order, they do not normally carry messages in opposition to that order.[2] Those who engage in terrorism do not operate within the acceptable parameters of accepted society, so the media rarely convey the existence of these groups' alternative views in their usual reporting. By undertaking acts of violence, terrorists hope to force their views into media outlets and thus obtain forums in which to expose and explain their beliefs and purposes. By providing demands, statements to be published, and interviews with reporters, terrorists hope to disseminate their message through the media and thus influence the public.

State terrorists operate with different purposes. Terrorist acts committed by governments and their surrogates are usually committed with the purposes of making the population acquiesce to the government's rule, destroying government opponents, and maintaining the power and policies of those currently in power. Although such acts are most often manifested in domestic situations, they can occur in international settings as well.

Terrorism as Warfare

Along with general and guerrilla warfare, terrorism can be viewed as one of three major forms of warfare available to strategists of violence.

General warfare occurs in international and national settings. International war normally involves one country against another in which the organized military forces of one government are pitted against the organized forces of another. Such warfare usually includes the use of armed forces against civilian targets in an enemy country and is illustrated by World War II, the Iran-Iraq war that was under way for nearly a decade in the 1980s, and the Gulf War, in which international forces liberated Kuwait from Iraq in 1991. In a national setting, general warfare is manifested as civil war, in which organized military forces battle other organized military forces in a conflict that encompasses much of the nation. Such internal warfare has been seen in the conflicts between Bangladesh (East Pakistan) and Pakistan in 1971, between Chinese communists and nationalists from 1927 to 1949, and between the nationalists and loyalists in the Spanish Civil War from 1936 to 1939.

Guerrilla warfare usually involves weaker armed forces against government armed forces and officials. This type of conflict is usually domestic but can spread into an international arena. Such warfare can be a prelude to civil war. The major characteristic of guerrilla warfare is that it is usually a prolonged internal conflict that encompasses most of a country, not merely a small region. For such a conflict to be successful, popular support must be available for the guerrillas, and the physical geography must be difficult for the government to control because of jungles, swamps, deserts, mountains, or other features that make conventional military operations by government forces difficult. This type of warfare is evident in the current conflicts in El Salvador and Afghanistan.

As a form of warfare, terrorism usually involves weak groups without much popular support pitted against government forces. It sometimes involves militarily weak groups with popular support against very strong government forces, as is the case in Lebanon, where Shi'ite Moslems have killed and taken hostage Western civilians whose governments have aligned themselves with Christian and Sunni Moslem factions, and in Germany, where the Red Army Faction has attacked NATO military facilities. In cases of state terrorism, government forces or their supporters or surrogates act against the population or dissidents. This is illustrated by the Guatemalan government's campaign against native Indians and others in the population who oppose the military-dominated government of that nation.

Acts and Extent of Terrorism

The manifestations of terrorism include a variety of violent acts. Various objectives can be met in whole or in part through these acts. The type of action helps determine which of the objectives are achieved. Common acts of nonstate terrorists include bombings (the most common type), shootings, arsons, hostage takings, and hijackings. Prolonged acts such as hijackings and kidnappings, in addition to promoting fear, often result in significant news coverage and the opportunity for media forums to be used for making political statements. Bombings, assassinations, and other condensed acts serve a variety of objectives but are not likely to result in the availability of public media forums.

Terrorism committed by governments commonly includes genocide, death squads, torture, concentration camps, mass starvation, expulsion, and forced relocation.

Although terrorism has been a major political and popular concern in recent years, that concern has far exceeded the extent of terrorist violence and reflects the effectiveness of terrorism in inducing fear and concern. About 700 to 800 incidents of international nonstate terrorism and about 2,500 incidents of domestic nonstate terrorism occur annually throughout the world. Few incidents occur in the United States, averaging only about two dozen annually in recent years. During the past two decades, about 45 percent of terrorist attacks have occurred in the Middle East, 20 percent in Latin America, 15 percent in Europe, and the rest elsewhere. No part of the world and no particular type of government is immune. Authoritarian states suffer terrorism, just as liberal democratic nations do. China and the formerly authoritarian states of the Soviet Union and Central and Eastern Europe have all suffered from shootings, bombings, and hijackings, but those occurrences are not well covered in Western media because of the lack of access and information.

About half of all victims of nonstate terrorism are government employees. Nearly 80 percent of those victims are diplomats, 15 percent are military personnel, and 5 percent are other government officials.[3] When nongovernment employees are involved, about one-quarter have been business executives. This was especially true during the 1960s and 1970s when European and Latin American organizations engaging in terrorism targeted business executives for kidnapping for ransom. That number has declined from its highpoint in the 1960s and 1970s due to social changes and effective security measures implemented by business firms and governments. As an occupational category, journalists are second only to business executives as nongovernmental targets of terrorism.

Although American citizens are often victims of terrorist attacks, they account for only about one-quarter of all terrorist victims. That number is high because Americans are often large-group victims of hijackings. When deaths from terrorist acts are considered, American citizens account for less than 5 percent of the total. In recent years, an average of 12 to 15 Americans have died each year from terrorist violence.[4] This number pales when compared to other causes of death. For example, 90 Americans die each year from being hit by lightning, 2,000 from gun accidents, 20,000 are murdered, and 25,000 die from drunken driving.

When state terrorism is involved, the primary victims—when specific individuals are singled out—are usually centrist and leftist political activists, human rights activists, educators, journalists, and students.

Although accurate international statistics are difficult to compile, most researchers accept data that indicates approximately ten thousand deaths have occurred in the past three decades due to nonstate terrorism. State terrorism has been responsible for three to seven million deaths during that time, depending upon whether one includes the Vietnam War in the data.

Causes of Terrorism

A variety of theories have been offered as to why individuals and groups resort to terrorism as a tactic to achieve their goals. These theories reflect the different approaches of those studying the phenomenon. One major approach argues that deprivation, oppression, and frustration result in terrorism as individuals strive to better their social conditions. A corollary argument is that terrorism arises when the rights of individuals are not protected and individuals persecuted by those with power react violently. A second school of thought embraces the view that terrorism arises when groups are unable to attain their goals through existing social and political structures. This occurs when minority or fringe groups or individuals are left out of effectual public participation by their own choice or the choice of others, or because their views are rejected by the greater mass of people. A third view holds that terrorism arises when government loses control of society and anarchy erupts.

Martha Crenshaw has argued that causes of terrorism fall into two distinct categories: preconditions and precipitants. The former group is comprised of conditions such as concrete grievances of minorities against majority elements of a population, the lack of opportunity for effective political participation, mass passivity, and a dissatisfied elite.

> Terrorism per se is not usually a reflection of mass discontent or deep cleavages in society. More often it represents the disaffection of a fragment of the elite, who may take it upon themselves to act on the behalf of a majority unaware of its plight, unwilling to take action to remedy grievances, or unable to express dissent. This discontent, however subjective in origin or minor in scope, is blamed on the government and its supporters.[5]

Crenshaw argues that this dissatisfied elite can be moved to acts of terrorism by precipitating events, occurrences that induce them to go beyond the bounds of normal social action. These events are not the reason for terrorism, of course, but are the final straw that leads to violent acts.[6]

Ted Robert Gurr has argued that the legitimacy and stability of governments play important roles in whether terrorism develops. He maintains that when governments are viewed as legitimate, violence against them and society at large is inhibited and that modern states thus experience less violence than developing states.[7]

State terrorism arises when governments and their supporters feel threatened by unrest within the populations of their nations or believe that external populations pose threats to the well-being or continued maintenance of the status quo. In such situations, governments employ violence to eradicate their enemies and to ensure acquiescence of the population in general. The impetus for such violence can be either a deliberate decision in the highest echelons of the government, or decisions made by lower-level military and security personnel to begin such actions on their own. In the latter case, higher authorities are often not consulted beforehand, but the continued operation of the terrorism campaign is dependent upon their acquiescence to the acts of violence and provision of support.

It is impossible, of course, to assert specific, widely generalizable, causes of terrorism because unique historical, political, economic, and religious environments and circumstances exist in every setting in which such violence takes place. It is clear, however, that when deep desires to significantly change existing social situations, to protect and promote the existing setting, or to promote and reestablish previous social relations are thwarted — or appear thwarted — anger and frustration can move individuals to embrace terrorism as a means for achieving their desired goals. Individuals and groups, however, also choose terrorism as a tactic by rational choice.

Why Terrorism Is Opposed

Most people regard terrorism as evil and immoral, but few take the time to consider why they feel this way. When asked to explain why, the reasons given vary. But two major concerns emerge in such discussions. First, terrorism threatens stability and the ability to govern. This is usually a major reason given by persons reflecting a military or political viewpoint. Second, terrorism results in death and injury to persons. This is cited by both civilians and government personnel as a major reason for opposing terrorism.

This second argument presents particular problems because few government officials and civilians completely reject violence as an acceptable means of achieving social and political goals. Although committed pacifists reject the death of persons for any purpose, their numbers are not great. Most persons are willing to permit some deaths, depending upon the situation. One way of questioning one's tolerance for violence is to ask whether one would accept, or would have accepted, the killing of Adolf Hitler, Joseph Stalin, Pol Pot, Ayatollah Ruholla Khomeini, Augusto Pinochet, or Saddam Hussein as justifiable. If one answers yes to any of these, then one believes there are times in which political violence that kills persons is warranted.

But what of killing innocent human beings? Although some are willing to accept the death of "evil" persons and even combatants, they bridle at terrorism as an acceptable means of achieving political and social goals because it involves the deaths of noncombatants. Stated tolerance for such deaths is low among most persons, but governments and the public have allowed considerations beyond the deaths of civilians to enter decisions about whether warfare is warranted, and those considerations have changed during the twentieth century as the technology and conventions of warfare have changed and made civilian deaths more "acceptable." In considering the percentage of military versus civilian casualties that have occurred in wars to which the United States was a party, one can trace the change in how civilians have been viewed as a legitimate part of warfare. In World War I civilians accounted for only 5 percent of all deaths. In World War II that amount rose to 48 percent. During the Korean War civilians accounted for 84 percent of all deaths, and in the Vietnam War civilians accounted for 90 percent. Clearly the rules of war and the acceptability of killing innocents have changed significantly during this century. It should not be shocking that disenfranchised and angry groups accept civilian deaths as one means of achieving their goals when governments do likewise.

The difficulties of casting aspersion on those who engage in political violence has been pointed out by Leon Baradat, who notes,

It is tempting for some people to conclude that those who would use violence to gain their political objectives are extremists. This, however, is not necessarily the case. True, violence is a major tool of certain extremist political groups. But violence is used by people at practically every point on the political spectrum. The death penalty, property expropriation, and warfare itself are examples of forms of violence supported by people distributed all along the political continuum. Thus it is unwise to jump to conclusions about the methods others use to accomplish their political goals.[8]

The fact that many individuals do not view the moral justification of terrorism similarly to the moral justification of violence committed by nations is problematic because it presents a duplicitous argument against the ends of violence justifying the means. C. A. J. Coady has pointed out that

many condemnations of terrorism are subject to the charge of inconsistency, if not hypocrisy, because they insist on applying one kind of morality to the state's use of violence in war . . . and another kind altogether to the use of violence by . . . the revolutionary. For one's own state a utilitarian standard is adopted which morally legitimates the intentional killing of noncombatants so that such acts of state terrorism as the bombing of Dresden are deemed to be morally sanctioned by the good ends they supposedly serve. The same people, however, make the move to higher ground when considering the activities of the rebel or the revolutionary and judge his killing of noncombatants [as evil and unjustifiable].[9]

Thus, rational consideration of the issue of terrorism forces individuals to choose between the complete rejection of violence as a means of achieving social and political ends and the acceptance of the less moral, utilitarian view that violence is acceptable in some circumstances. Most who accept the latter view try to evaluate the use of violence based on (1) social and legal distinctions and sanctions that permit and prohibit some individuals to use violence, (2) acceptable and unacceptable victims of violence, and (3) tolerable and intolerable levels of violence. This allows them to define the violence they accept and perpetrate as more moral than the violence of others.

The result of this utilitarian approach is that terrorist violence opposed by individuals and nations is attacked out of self-interest and perceived lack of justification and not out of a coherent philosophical position. Consequently, agreement on what violence is appropriate and inappropriate is impossible and the hope of widespread international agreement to end terrorism is a fantasy.

Approaches to the Study of Terrorism

Serious study of terrorism has been underway for only about three decades, and much of the literature in the field is descriptive, speculative, and polemical, based on case studies and conjecture about the motives, causes, and effects of terrorism. Most of the existing scholarship lacks the detachment of social science because government and politics have been the major emphases of what has been written. Most of the literature focuses on the effects of terrorism on governments, and on public policy aspects for controlling terrorism. Much of the research has been done by military and government personnel, their consultants, or political scientists with a government orientation.

Significant study of the phenomenon using social science techniques has been undertaken for only about a decade. In the 1980s, more detached scholars and critics of the government-oriented approach began to explore the subject. Their work has added new perspectives to discussion of the topic, but it has not yet yielded definitive scholarly work on the subject. The work of these "objective" scholars takes place in an unfriendly environment because it challenges and sometimes offends the views of government, media, and other terrorism scholars who have accepted the traditional government-oriented approach or have policy interests that they wish to protect.

The literature on terrorism is varied. Popular literature includes books and articles designed to sell to a wide audience and tends to be jingoistic and propagandistic because the material is designed to influence and persuade. Information in most popular literature is subject to interpretations and presentations designed to suit expedience or polemical purposes. Examples of such literature include Claire Sterling's *The Terror Network: The Secret War of International Terrorism* (New York: Holt, Rinehart, and Winston, 1980), which in a Cold War approach blamed the Soviet Union for most of the world's violence and was written with the support of the Central Intelligence Agency; and an opposing view found in Edward S. Herman's *The Real Terror Network: Terrorism in Fact and Propaganda* (Boston: South End Press, 1982). Herman's book considers right-wing- and government-sponsored acts of terrorism and explores U.S. ties to acts worldwide.

A second approach to the subject emphasizes tactical aspects. This military and police approach provides information on how to respond to specific incidents and different types of incidents and how to stop the spread of terrorism. Some of this material is classified, but publicly available examples of this literature include Abraham Miller, *Terrorism and Hostage Negotiation* (Boulder, Colo.: Westview Press, 1980); Steven

Sloan, *Simulating Terrorism* (Norman: University of Oklahoma Press, 1981); and G. Wardlaw, *Political Terrorism: Theory, Tactics, and Countermeasures* (London: Cambridge University Press, 1982).

A related government and political approach deals with how terrorism affects public policy and political power, the political and military efforts that can be used to halt terrorism, and appropriate responses from a political standpoint. Examples include Yonah Alexander et al., eds., *Terrorism: Theory and Practice* (Boulder, Colo.: Westview Press, 1979); Yonah Alexander et al., eds., *Control of Terrorism* (New York: Crane, Rusak, 1979); Benjamin Netanyahu, ed., *Terrorism: How the West Can Win* (New York: Farrar, Straus, Giroux, 1986); and Michael Stohl, ed., *The Politics of Terrorism*, 3d ed. (New York: Marcel Dekker, 1988). Significant contributions have also been made in this area by Paul Wilkinson, Brian Jenkins, Daniel Bell, and Richard Clutterbuck. These government/political topics account for the largest portion of the available literature.

A significant psychological and sociological approach is concerned with what goes on in the mind of terrorists and the effects terrorism has on terrorist groups and the public. The literature of this approach is generally limited to articles by psychologists and psychiatrists, but some book literature is appearing, most notably Yonah Alexander and John Gleason, eds., *Behavioral and Quantitative Perspectives on Terrorism* (New York: Pergamon, 1980). Another aspect of this approach includes studies of how victims are affected physically and mentally, how the acts of violence affect families and friends, and how therapists can help victims and their families after incidents are over.

A significant body of literature approaches terrorism from a legal perspective. This research explores the use of domestic and international law against perpetrators, promotes the development of new laws and treaties against acts of terrorism, and studies the effectiveness of such laws. Important contributions to this literature include M. Cherif Bassiouni, *International Terrorism and Political Crime* (Springfield, Ill.: Charles C Thomas, 1975) and Robert A. Friedlander, *Terrorism: Documents of International and Local Control* (Dobbs Ferry, N.Y.: Oceana Publications, 1979).

A communication approach, considering terrorism as a form of communication and the possibility of communication as a contagion of terrorism, has developed during the last decade. Material in this literature concerns how coverage of terrorism affects public policy, the public, and terrorists. Few significant books on the topic are available, but important contributions include Alex P. Schmid and Janny de Graaf, *Violence as Communication: Insurgent Terrorism and the Western News*

Media (Beverly Hills, Calif.: Sage Publications, 1982); Philip Schlesinger et al., *Televising "Terrorism": Political Violence in Popular Culture* (London: Comedia, 1983); Richard Clutterbuck, *The Media and Political Violence* (London: Macmillan, 1983); and Abraham Miller, *Terrorism, the Media and the Law* (Dobbs Ferry, N.Y.: Transnational, 1982). These books outline criticism and some of the problems of communication in an important fashion but are limited by regional and political/legal biases and the lack of research or data to support or refute many of their propositions. Nevertheless, these seminal works provide important departures for contemporary research.

Other literature, mostly speculative or based on isolated case studies, uses the approaches outlined in the general study of terrorism. Few of those articles or chapters contain significant contributions because most are rhetorical and polemical and promote specific policies or viewpoints. Notable in this regard are Michael P. O'Neill's *Terrorist Spectaculars: Should TV Coverage Be Curbed?* (New York: Priority Press, 1986); Sarah Midgley and Virginia Rice, eds., *Terrorism and the Media in the 1980s* (Washington, D.C.: The Media Institute, 1984); and *Terrorism and the Media* (Washington, D.C.: American Legal Foundation, n.d.). In the past decade, however, a growing body of more important research is appearing that studies how coverage has affected politics and public policy and how it has affected victims and their families. Other studies have explored just what information is conveyed in coverage. And still others have focused on the rhetorical aspects of the reportage. Examples of these studies are found in Yonah Alexander and Robert G. Picard, eds., *In the Camera's Eye: News Coverage of Terrorist Events* (Washington, D.C.: Brassey's, 1991) and A. Odasuo Alali and Kenoye Kelvin Eke, eds., *Media Coverage of Terrorism: Methods of Diffusion* (Newbury Park, Calif.: Sage, 1991).

Although these contributions to the literature of terrorism and the role of media and communication in the phenomena provide information and some perspective on the issue of how media portray terrorism and terrorists, they do not provide readers with a comprehensive approach to communication aspects of the issue or understanding of the issues and current state of knowledge about media aspects of terrorism. This book attempts to do that and will consider the social context of that communication, criticism and problems associated with the coverage, the accuracy and bases for the criticisms, and means of dealing with those criticisms that are warranted.

3

The Setting and Types of Communication in Terrorism

TERRORISM DOES NOT TAKE PLACE in a contextual vacuum. The violence and its messages must be considered in terms of the social settings in which it takes place. These messages cannot be separated from their socio-institutional contexts and from their own effects on influencing, altering, or strengthening those settings. In addition, the variety of types of communication that take place surrounding terrorist events must be considered to fully understand the role of institutions and media in acts of terrorism.

Socio-institutional Contexts

Institutions of society determine, reflect, and perpetuate the norms and values of a given society. Those values in many ways define the type of society that exists through the emphases placed on various values and norms. Media are one of the primary institutions of society and play significant roles in transmitting and perpetuating dominant values of a society and permitting other institutions to communicate with the populace. In modern societies, these other institutions include the state, that is, government apparatuses; the church, that is, religious institutions;

and the business/financial complex. The major noninstitutional factor in these societies is the populace.

To understand the salience of terrorism, it is necessary to understand the interplay between these institutions and the populace and how terrorists attempt to alter or support those relationships. Figure 3.1 outlines the socio-institutional context of *external* terrorism. In this type of conflict, perpetrators from other nations or societies, or those originally from within the society who have completely rejected the existing social relations, seek to alter the society by forcing fundamental and profound social change that rearranges relations among institutions and the populace. The four major institutions and the populace, although separate, are encompassed within and operate as portions of the society. The perpetrators of terrorism in this setting, however, operate outside the social system.

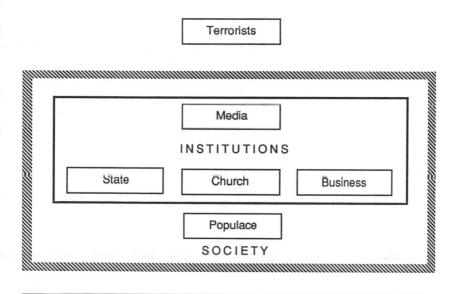

3.1. The socio-institutional
context of external terrorism.

Terrorism in this type of social setting is illustrated by the activities of social-revolutionary groups that seek progressive change to new and different social relations and international terrorist groups that attempt to punish and change the behavior of other societies. Groups engaging in this type of external terrorism include the Baader-Meinhoff group and its offshoots, which reject and target the government and financial institutions and class relations of German society. The Mau-Mau attacks in Kenya during the 1950s, which sought to end British colonial domination by attacking Europeans and their property in that nation, are also an example of this type of terrorism, as are the more contemporary examples of international terrorist activities in France, Britain, and Germany by Moslem fundamentalists linked to Hezbollah and Islamic Jihad.

The second socio-institutional context, *internal* terrorism, is outlined in Figure 3.2. In this type of conflict, perpetrators from within the society engage in acts of social/political violence. Several types of terrorism take place in this type of situation. First, it is the setting in which perpetrators who have not rejected all the institutions or social relations of the existing society, but who want to alter the social balance to change the control of institutions or establish a separate society, operate. Examples of this type of terrorism include the activities of Puerto Rican nationalists who attack the state institution of the United States.

Second, it is this internal context in which state terrorism occurs. In such cases the violent acts are committed by individuals or groups who are linked to or a part of the state institution, and the violence is most often perpetrated to preserve the existing distribution of power and control or promote policy interests. Examples of this include the French government's efforts to reduce opposition to nuclear testing in the South Pacific by bombing the Greenpeace ship, *Rainbow Warrior,* and the assassinations of exiled government opponents worldwide by Libyan security forces.

Finally, the internal setting describes situations in which reactionary terrorism occurs. This is the type of violence that seeks to return social relations to something that previously existed. Such terrorism is illustrated by the activities of the Moslem Brotherhood in Egypt, which wishes to lessen the secular influence of the government and business institutions.

Describing terrorism in these terms helps develop understanding of violence as part of a social system. This structural-functionalist view — developed out of the work of Herbert Spencer, Emile Durkheim, Robert Merton, and Talcott Parsons — maintains that all social systems seek stability by attempting to locate a point at which the institutions and popu-

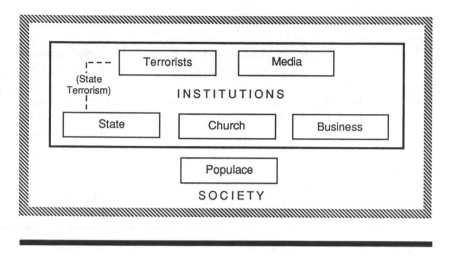

**3.2. The socio-institutional
context of internal terrorism.**

lace come to terms regarding their various roles and the distribution of
power among the interrelated parts of the society.[1] When a consensus is
reached on these issues, the existing society becomes legitimized. Although this legitimization does not mean that the society is necessarily
the best possible one or that everyone is pleased with the arrangements,
it does indicate that the majority of the populace and the institutions
accept the roles, positions, and power distributions in the society and
acquiesce to them.

Once legitimization occurs, the institutions attempt to maintain this
position of stability or status quo. Structural stability requires general
agreement of all the institutions on the basic values and norms of the
society and requires that the public accept that generalized view.[2] The
institutions are never fully independent. They influence, and are influenced by, each other and the populace. If the institutions conflict,
stability diminishes. Although small conflicts regularly occur, significant
disagreements are infrequent. If conflict between institutions and the
populace exists, the society cannot continue to be stable, and this leads

to conditions that result in revolution, civil war, or other significant social change.

Media, as a social institution, are subject to the same forces of interdependence as other institutions, and their values and norms must remain within the parameters of the generalized values and norms of the society in which they operate. Thus, according to J. Herbert Altschull, media are "agents of power" in whatever society they exist.[3] As a result, media regularly exclude ideas and values that conflict with those predominantly held in the society and do not provide access to those individuals and groups that are on the fringe of society or that hold ideas and values alien to the society. Because media support the values and norms of their society, those kept from communicating through media channels can turn to violence, argues Neil C. Livingstone: "In view of the inability of most terrorist organizations to disseminate their message through conventional mass media, terrorists have sought instead to create news in order to communicate their existence, ideas, and power to the general public, cognizant that established news organizations will report their actions and deeds for them."[4]

In this institutional setting, media act both as relatively passive communication channels and as active communicators. When relatively passive, media convey the views of others without deliberately adding significant meaning of their own. This, however, does not mean that no such meaning is added, because professional social norms and values enter the process of selecting, reporting, and packaging the news. This type of influence on the meaning is usually not deliberate, and most often media personnel are not aware they are adding meaning to the facts. They believe, instead, that their "objectivity" protects them from adding meaning. Media can also become active communicators, specifically conveying the views of reporters, editors, and media owners, sometimes along with the views of others. In addition, media personnel both knowingly and unknowingly add significant meaning based on their own values, beliefs, and perceptions, and the influences of the other institutions and populace.

In covering terrorism, media can passively carry news of the events and the views of terrorists, government officials, and others, or they can become active communicators, taking part in the situation, bringing other views and meaning to the situation, or conveying them in their coverage.

The major goals of nonstate terrorists are to destabilize society and to exploit the resulting instability for their purposes. They do so by seeking to alter the relations between social institutions and the populace. Terrorists seek to redistribute power among institutions and the populace, and in doing so to change behavior of institutions. A primary means of accomplishing these goals is to establish conflict between institutions and disrupt their normal operations, thus bringing about instability and delegitimization.

A significant tactic for bringing institutions into conflict is to force change on the society or to make the populace fear demands for change. Because modern societies seek to maintain the status quo, they resist efforts to impose rapid or significant change and will use force to maintain that status quo. The ability of different social systems to assimilate change varies widely. Some societies are more resistant to change because they are less open to new ideas. Others, however, do not perceive and experience change as necessarily threatening. But such societies are few, and they usually will not accept all change, especially when it involves the structure of the society or significant redistributions of power. When deep conflict exists and force is used, the institutions of society might take differing approaches to the issues presented and, thus, important divisions can occur among institutions and bring instability to the system.

The importance of conflict as a factor and agent of social change has long been recognized. As early as the fourteenth century, Ibn Khaldun, the Arab scholar, argued that conflict was the basic mechanism for achieving social change throughout history.[5] The idea that conflict is a driving force for change was later embraced by Herbert Spencer, who argued that conflict brings evolutionary change in existing societies.[6]

In pursuit of their objectives of promoting change and bringing institutions into conflict, nonstate terrorists attack institutions as well as the populace. The most attacked institutions are the state, the business-financial complex, and the media. If terrorists create significant instability, the consensus and acquiescence of the population to the society might diminish, and delegitimization might occur. In cases of state terrorism, dissidents and the population are usually targeted rather than institutions. If the dissidents are strategically located within institutions and use those institutions in opposition to the state, however, the state terrorists might target those institutions.

Communication in Terrorist Events

Most observers of terrorism understand and assert the role of communication in terrorism and that such political violence is ineffectual if its existence is not conveyed to authorities, the populace, or terrorist supporters. Unless awareness of the act is developed in target audiences, acts of terrorism are useless as symbolic or destabilizing acts. Media are, of course, a significant tool for communicating about these events, and the actions of media in covering terrorism have been regularly discussed and criticized.

Although the media play a real and important role in conveying information about terrorism, many observers ignore the significance of other aspects and forms of communication in their discussions. Terror can and has been spread by word of mouth. Messages inherent in violence and events never reported in media can and have conveyed meaning to authorities and the public. Ignoring other important forms of communication about terrorism unduly colors understanding of the importance of media coverage as an effect of political violence. It gives the false impression that the messages terrorists wish to send and their effects could be halted if media did not cover acts of terrorism or if they altered that coverage significantly.

Communication is, of course, the process of acquiring and conveying information and assigning meaning to that information. It takes place in all terrorist events, whether small- or large-scale. Communication takes place between terrorists and their supporters, between government officials, between victims and observers, and between media and audiences. The communication process links persons and institutions in a system, making it possible to organize society and for any society to survive. As a result, the systems analysis approach to analyzing the role of communication in society is clearly applicable to communication in terrorist events. This methodological approach, called general system theory, developed in the natural sciences as researchers attempted to find a framework within which to explain behavior and relations among organisms and chemical substances, but has since been accepted within the social sciences where it has become a congenial partner to the social systems ideas of Spencer, Durkheim, and Parsons. The basis of this general systems approach includes work by Ludwig von Bertalanffy, James G. Miller, and others, in which they argue that phenomena usually exist in specific relations among a set of entities and that by analyzing those entities and relations one can employ deductive reasoning to predict and explain behavior. The entities and their relations thus constitute a system that can be analyzed as a whole or as separate parts of the whole.[7]

In communication systems, each individual operates with some autonomy but is a part of the whole social system and is influenced by other individuals and institutions in that system. At the same time, the individual participant has a reciprocal influence on these other individuals and institutions. Thus, change in one part of the social system affects other parts, and communication is the primary initiator and facilitator of this process.

The communication process is continual and unpreventable. It is dynamic because the participants in the process are always changing functions and there is no completely fixed sequence for the change. David Berlo describes the fluctuating situation as follows: "If we accept the concept of process, we view the events and relationships as dynamic, on-going, ever-changing, continuous. When we label something as a process we also mean that it does not have a beginning, an end, a fixed sequence of events. It is not static, at rest. It is moving. The ingredients within a process interact; each affects all of the others."[8]

It is in this constant conveyance and acquisition of information that individuals, groups, institutions, and society itself assign meaning to occurrences. Meaning is constructed by individuals, influenced by their relations with other persons and institutions, and they, in turn, influence these other persons and institutions. This process occurs on four important communication levels: (1) intrapersonal, (2) interpersonal, (3) organizational, and (4) mass.

Intrapersonal communication is that which is internal to individuals. In this type of communication, personal values, attitudes, background, perception, and patterns of thought come into play in interpreting and assigning meaning to information and events and in influencing individual behavior.

The internal process is also influenced by interpersonal communication, in which interaction with other individuals has an influence on that meaning. The forms in which these communications take place are not as formally structured as are organizational and mass communication because the formats of the communication, the forms of the messages, and the senses used to convey and receive the messages are not dictated by the highly formalized channels found in television, radio, newspapers, and magazines. As a result, interpersonal communication is not subject to as much direct control by organizations and institutions as is mass communication using media. This is not to say that interpersonal communication does not have structure or that rules about the forms of messages, their contexts, their contents, and how they are conveyed are missing. These influences on the interpersonal communication, however, can be controlled only indirectly by social institutions, and much of the control exists because of institutions' ability to propagate and maintain attitudes and beliefs. If media coverage of terrorist events were fully restrained by society, interpersonal communication would still convey the existence of such acts and assign meaning to them. Thus, interpersonal communication has a significant influence on attitudes, perceptions, and behavior that has been of interest to researchers.

Organizational and mass communication differ from intrapersonal and interpersonal communication in that they generally rely upon formalized, well-structured means of communication and communication directed toward the members of the organizations or the mass audiences. Mass media communication is the central means for large-scale society to communicate among its members; society could not continue to maintain itself without the communication ability offered by mass communication.

At the mass communication level, messages are normally verbal and visual, but, as in other levels, messages need not always be verbal or written. Nonverbal communications, such as signs, nonverbal sounds, and symbolic acts, also take place and are assigned significant meaning by communicators and observers. Visual images, notable omission of communication, gestures, and other nonverbal behavior all can convey meaning and are often important in conveying attitudes of communicators.

Communication during terrorist events takes place on all four major levels and is both verbal and nonverbal. The ability to inhibit or constrain communication in such events is limited because the four levels cannot be equally controlled. Although organizational and mass communication can be inhibited and constrained to some degree, experience has shown that they cannot be fully controlled by authorities. The shah of Iran, for example, while in full authoritarian control of the main communication media in that country, was unable to control the dissemination of revolutionary ideas by the Ayatollah Khomeini who made extensive use of tape-recorded messages smuggled into the country. In South Africa, after government banned oppositional media and forbade other media to report on antigovernment activities in 1987, oppositional groups placed "human radios" on buses carrying black workers to work. These individuals told of news about violence and government repression that was gathered both internally by a network of unofficial reporters and from other nations by listening to shortwave radio broadcasts. Clandestine radio stations operate in areas of conflict throughout the world, with significant operations supporting the contras in Nicaragua and the Democratic Revolutionary Front in El Salvador, and Palestinians in the West Bank and Israel.[9]

Intrapersonal and interpersonal communication are impossible to control because the lack of technology and the scale of society make it impossible to monitor individual thought, conversations, and letters.

Communication of terrorist events does not always involve mass communication, although much terrorism is clearly reported in media. But many events are not reported and some are reported only briefly. In these instances, intrapersonal, interpersonal, and organizational communication still take place so communication about the occurrences still takes place.

Constraints on the flow of information about terrorist acts and groups include direct and indirect censorship by authorities and the import placed on events by media, which is influenced by the type of occurrence, the location of the event, and the identity of victims. Local media and media in nations whose citizens suffer from terrorism generally convey the most information about terrorist events if government or other institutions or factors do not constrain their ability to do so.

At the intrapersonal level, knowledge of terrorist events exists for perpetrators, victims, and witnesses even if mass communication does not take place. These individuals organize, interpret, use, and assign meaning and import to the events internally and develop attitudes about the events, those involved in them, and the causes the activities promote. For perpetrators, this usually involves ego gratification and self-aggrandizement. For surviving victims and witnesses, this normally includes interpretation of events as a threat to survival and thus the creation of fear, anxiety, and disorientation.

Interpersonal communication about terrorist events takes place between individuals. This involves the creation and sharing of frames of references through which the events are interpreted. In the case of perpetrators, this results in the gratification of group ego and development of high morale as an effectual organization. Among the populace, those who are aware of the event convey it to others, along with their reactions. As persons jointly interpret terrorist events, the interpretation is generally negative, and fear is spread. This type of communication takes place whether or not mass media cover the events at all or limit the coverage of the events, but the amount of communication at the interpersonal level is heightened when certain incidents or groups are raised on the interpersonal agenda by media coverage.

Organizational communication also takes place in terrorist events. In terrorist groups themselves, communication of the event can take place between cells or separated portions of the organization. Reports about the attack are circulated, and discussions of its impact and effectiveness might be held. Organizational communication also takes place in the targeted government as it attempts to react and cope with terrorism and discusses implications, potential responses, policy issues, and effectiveness of its operations.

When reporting of events of terrorism takes place in the media, a significant and sometimes complex flow of communication is established. The flow involves both one- and two-way communication. One-way flow of information is that which does not involve immediate reaction or discussion between the participants in the communication. Two-way flow involves interactive communication between participants in which such discussion can take place.

The flow of communication in reported acts of terrorism is outlined in Figure 3.3. The flow initiates with the act of violence and conveyance of its occurrence to media. The act is reported by media to the targeted populace, targeted government(s), other terrorist groups and supporters, and other governments. The response of the targeted government is then communicated to media, which report the response to their audiences. The amount of flow varies for each incident, with the import given incidents by media and government being primary influences on the amount of coverage provided.

If events are ongoing, additional types of communication might take place. The targeted government might attempt to communicate through the media to the perpetrating group, an action sometimes called *media diplomacy*. The targeted government might attempt to avoid the inefficiencies of media diplomacy through direct communication with the perpetrating group. In addition, the targeted government might communicate with nontargeted governments, or other terrorist groups or group supporters, asking them to serve as intermediaries with the perpetrating group or to exert influence.

The socio-institutional context of terrorism also influences the types of communication that take place during and surrounding terrorist events. In situations involving external terrorism, media of the country attacked are likely to diminish or belittle the actions, and media of uninvolved countries are likely to ignore the event or convey very little information about it. In external terrorism, it is also likely that communication between targeted and nontargeted governments, perpetrators and supporters, nontargeted governments and terrorist supporters, and nontargeted governments and media will take place. In the context of internal terrorism, however, these communications with other governments and terrorist supporters generally do not take place. Media reporting on internal terrorism in their own country are likely to diminish its import while providing significant amounts of coverage that attempt to explain the events as means of preserving social stability. The media are also disposed to engage in media diplomacy in such situations, but governments may choose to directly communicate with the perpetrating group.

In considering the importance of the various types of communica-

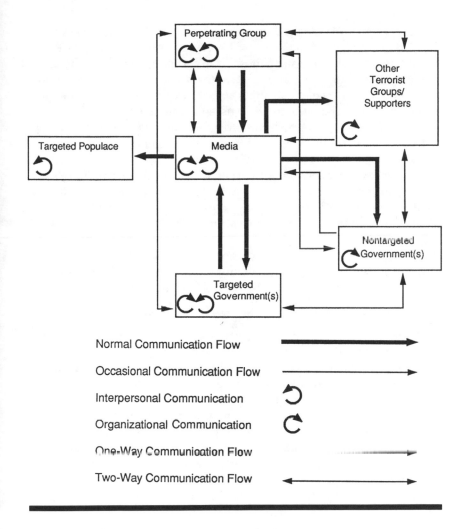

Normal Communication Flow

Occasional Communication Flow

Interpersonal Communication

Organizational Communication

One-Way Communication Flow

Two-Way Communication Flow

3.3. Communication flow in reported terrorist acts.

tion and flows of communication about terrorist events, several approaches can be applied to the roles of media in terrorism: (1) the behavioral approach, which considers how people and institutions respond to communications and the effects of communications on their behavior and attitudes; (2) the cognitive approach, which explores how communication affects the thoughts of persons and leaders of institutions and groups; and (3) the media environment approach, which focuses on how media affect society by their existence and conveyance of information and news.

The behavioral approach provides several avenues of inquiry related to issues of terrorism. The first is stimulus-response theory, which was popular from the 1920s to the 1940s. This theory grew out of the belief that well-crafted messages (stimuli) would elicit desired responses from audiences.[10] Many who are not well schooled in communication theory and research attempt to significantly apply this view, arguing that acts of terrorism (stimuli) are conveyed through media channels, immediately resulting in the desired effects of persuasion and/or fear (response). However, communication scholars do not significantly embrace this theory because it has never been shown to work as hypothesized despite significant amounts of research. The major reason for the failure of the stimulus-response theory to be shown as an important means of affecting audiences was identified as its inability to accommodate the significant individual differences that exist among members of mass audiences.[11] A review of the terrorism literature shows no evidence that this theory is any more successful in explaining communication about terrorism than it was in affecting audiences in other types of communication.

With the rejection of stimulus-response theory as an explanation for communications effects, many communication scholars turned to the two-step flow theory. This theory holds that messages conveyed through media influence the attitudes and ideas of opinion leaders. These opinion leaders then engage in interpersonal communication with members of the public—passing on information and their interpretation of that information—that helps to shape attitudes and opinions of the populace at large.[12] This approach, which has significant support from evidence in communication research, can be applied to the issue of communication and terrorism by exploring first the effects of terrorism on opinion leaders and then the messages these leaders convey to the populace as a whole.

A particularly salient area of behavioral research involves the effects of media portrayals of violence. Although no one seriously maintains that reporting terrorism will lead average citizens to commit such acts, concerns over the effects of coverage on disenfranchised and angry persons and groups have been raised. Three communication-of-violence theories are particularly germane: (1) stimulating effects, which postulates that violence portrayed in media — especially on television — might psychologically stimulate those already inclined toward violent acts; (2) observational learning, which holds that individuals can learn violent behavior by observing it; and (3) reinforcement, which holds that observing violence in media can reinforce existing predispositions to violence. These theories, although providing significant avenues for inquiries about terrorism and media, have not yet been significantly applied to the field.

Relevant cognitive approaches to communication effects include the importance of intrapersonal, interpersonal, and mass communication in developing attitudes about terrorism and terrorists and constructing reality. The ways in which cognitive processes work together to affect perception, consciousness, memory, and attitudes at the intrapersonal and interpersonal level have been explored by a number of researchers, but little research applying these approaches to communication about terrorism has yet been completed.

Several important approaches to understanding how individuals' attitudes and behavior are affected when differing values, beliefs, and attitudes conflict could be used to provide better understanding of why individuals support some violence but reject other violence: (1) the balance model, which argues that when a person's attitudes toward objects or persons conflict, the individual will seek to rebalance them by selecting between attitudes or beliefs; (2) the congruity approach, which maintains that when intrapersonal conflict occurs, the individual will compromise and reduce the strength of acceptance of one of the conflicting attitudes; (3) the dissonance approach, which asserts that when behavior, attitudes, and beliefs are brought into conflict, individuals will seek to reduce the dissonance by justification and ignoring or avoiding situations and information that create dissonance; and (4) coorientation theory, which observes that when individuals have regular interpersonal communications, each strives to develop harmony between personal beliefs and attitudes, perception of the other's beliefs and attitudes, and affinity for the other individual. In doing so, each person selects between alternative attitudes and behaviors, discarding or ignoring those in conflict with the attitudes and behaviors of the other individual.[13]

The cognitive approach also involves the idea that messages conveyed in media help construct the way in which the world is perceived. Institutional influences on media and the media influence on audiences help them construct reality. This construction of reality, however, is not totally in the control of communicators because individual members of media audiences limit its reception and retention through internal mechanisms of selective perception, selective exposure, and selective retention. These cognitive approaches have been receiving attention in recent years, and studies indicate that significant meaning is achieved by constructing specific "realities" about terrorism that support the status quo. This aspect of media portrayals of terrorism will be discussed in Chapters 6 and 7.

The media environment approach provides three important theories that have bearing on media aspects of terrorism. The first is agenda setting, which postulates that media are not very efficient at influencing the attitudes of their audiences but have a significant ability to influence what topics or issues audiences think about.[14] People accept media ideas and issues as important and worthy of their concern. Thus, coverage makes events and topics salient. A second media environment theory, status conferral, holds that persons and groups gain status and become viewed as important when they are covered by the media. The mere fact of coverage, the selection of these groups or persons from among the numerous groups and persons competing for attention, thus serves as a means of elevating their status to one worthy of the public's concern or attention. Finally, the cultivation theory provides the idea that significant coverage of violence in news and dramatic portrayals of violence in media cultivate audience fears and concerns about the world. These approaches are beginning to generate interest among scholars, and a number of studies have begun to provide evidence on these issues, as will be discussed in Chapters 6 and 7.

Before turning to the issues of how terrorism is covered, its meaning, and its implications, we need to consider the role of communication in persuasion and the applicability of persuasive techniques to terrorist communication. We will then turn to the issue of how government views this communication and the conflicts that occur with media in handling the messages.

4

Persuasive Communication and Terrorism

ACTS OF NONSTATE TERRORISM are designed to influence a society by creating conditions in which change can be induced in the behavior of social institutions or in the power distribution among institutions or between institutions and the populace. Because these acts of violence are designed to produce effects and influence attitudes and behavior, they should be considered as forms of persuasive communication.

Martha Crenshaw has noted that "terrorist violence communicates a political message; its ends go beyond damaging an enemy's material resources. The victims or objects of the terrorist group have little intrinsic value to the terrorist group but represent a larger human audience whose reaction the terrorists seek."[1]

Communication can be analyzed on a continuum running from purely mental activity to purely physical activity. It is not confined to only specifically crafted verbal, written, or visual messages but includes gestures, actions, and any other activity that conveys meaning. It has been observed that

> as a term of communication behavior, terrorism has the unusual function of operating at both ends of the continuum. Propaganda, diplomacy, advertising, persuasion, education — all operate exclusively at the verbal or mental end. Violence, force, torture, and third degree abuse use physical means to attain their objectives. Terrorism and brainwash-

ing are initiated for communication purposes at the mental end, but are escalated, as the communication progresses, to the physical end of the continuum.[2]

The utility of acts of terrorism as communicative acts has increased as the scale of modern society has broken down social ties and traditional communication channels and replaced them with media intended to convey messages to large audiences across large distances. Without such media, groups and individuals wishing to communicate in large societies or transnational situations would be faced with nearly insurmountable difficulties of being heard because of the large number of persons in the audience and the distances between members of the audience and the communicators. The development of mass circulation print media in the nineteenth century and the rise of electronic media in the twentieth century have made it possible to break down these barriers of time and space. The one-way nature of communication using mass media, however, has created a passive audience that merely receives information and entertainment rather than interacting with it. In recent decades, the passivity has been compounded by the increasing number of media competing for audience attention. As a result, even the most mainstream communicators regularly jolt, titillate, and play on the emotions of audiences to gain that attention.

All political communicators who do not directly control or operate media regularly compete to gain access to media or media attention that can be used to explain and convey their views to the mass audiences. Media formats and programming, however, limit the ability of even individuals operating within the structures of the society to have access, and media generally carry only the views of the most prominent political individuals and the dominant views of the society. When less prominent political communicators are unable to immediately gain attention, they often resort to tactics including demonstrations and civil disobedience to gain coverage in news shows that will carry reports on such activities and their causes.

Individuals who have rejected a society or who are challenging its legitimacy from within, or from other nations, are often completely blocked in their attempts, even in generally accepted forms, to gain coverage. When such groups become frustrated and more disenfranchised, some choose violence to communicate that frustration and attract attention to their cause, thus seeking to change attitudes and behavior.

When authorities respond to nonstate terrorism, they also employ efforts to influence the populace through persuasive techniques intended to counteract the messages conveyed by terrorists. In doing so, officials hope to mobilize public opinion against the terrorists' causes and actions and to gain support for retaliatory government actions. In situations where authorities engage in or support terrorism against the population or a foreign enemy, they employ the rhetoric of violence to convey messages just as do nonstate terrorists.

Because terrorist actions are designed to promote attitudinal and behavioral change, terrorist acts need to be considered as a form of persuasive communication. The separate functions and roles of persuasion, propaganda, and publicity have bearing on terrorist violence; the principles of those techniques can be applied to terrorism.

Terrorism and Persuasion

Persuasion involves communicative acts designed to create attitudes, public opinion, and psychological environments that are conducive to the accomplishment of objectives of particular causes, persons, or organizations. A variety of techniques are used to promote the interests of the communicator over the interests of others. Hugh Rank has noted that most persuasive efforts attempt to intensify or downplay aspects of a cause, person, or institution in that subject's interest. His schema of persuasion reveals how persuasion techniques are used in such efforts (Figure 4.1).[3]

Intensification refers to efforts that emphasize good points of a cause or bad points of competitors or opponents in order to gain support for one's position. Techniques that serve this effort include (1) repetition, the continual restatement of major points or arguments; (2) association, linking the cause to something positive or placing it in opposition to something negative; and (3) composition, the casting of messages in an environment that emphasizes the goodness of the cause through background visuals, music, and other evocative elements that bring on an emotional response to support the cause of the communicator.

Downplaying, on the other hand, involves attempts to not deal with particular aspects. This is accomplished through noncommunication or de-emphasis of negative points about the subject or any good points about competitors' or opponents' positions. Techniques of downplaying are (1) omission, not telling the whole story or employing euphemisms to avoid words that would force one to confront negative aspects; (2) diversion, taking the audience's minds off real issues or characteristics of the

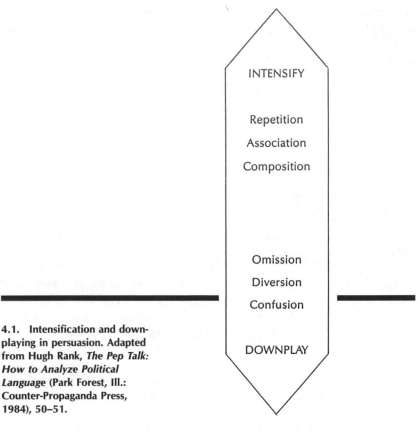

4.1. Intensification and downplaying in persuasion. Adapted from Hugh Rank, *The Pep Talk: How to Analyze Political Language* (Park Forest, Ill.: Counter-Propaganda Press, 1984), 50–51.

subject by employing devices such as humor or belittlement, or raising red herrings that distract attention; and (3) confusion, misunderstanding that is deliberately promoted by using detailed information, jargon, and contradictory information to overwhelm and confuse the public about the facts.

The purpose of employing persuasive tactics is to develop public opinion that helps a cause, person, or organization. Major goals of persuasion are to neutralize hostile opinions so that a cause is no longer opposed, to change hostile opinions into favorable ones that support the cause, to change neutral opinions into favorable ones, and to maintain favorable opinions that previously existed.

The difficulties of affecting public opinion have long been recognized, and a number of major principles involving the ability to alter public opinion were established as early as the 1940s.[4] Among these are the principles that opinion is highly sensitive to important events and that such events, more than persuasive words, induce change. A corollary principle is that temporary swings from one extreme position to another can occur as the result of events of unusual magnitude; such arousal, however, is usually short-term. Self-interest has been established as being more important than any other factor in the determination of public opinion. If self-interest is clear, opinions already established are difficult to change.[5]

During times of crisis, public opinion has been shown to swing to support leaders, with leadership receiving greater support in such times than at any other time. But the public has also been shown to expect more of their leaders in those moments. Leaders who fail to evidence appropriate decisiveness, resolve, courage, and understanding find that public opinion can quickly turn against them and thus add new difficulties to times of crisis.

The concept of persuasion is important in discussing terrorism because perpetrators of terroristic political violence clearly try to influence society and create attitudes supportive of their positions. Terrorism, however, does not fall into the normal persuasion paradigm. Its associative and composition techniques conflict with the values of intensification outlined by Rank, and few attempts to downplay negative aspects of terrorist acts are made by perpetrators. In fact, most terrorists intend to promote these aspects. These difficulties in classifying terrorism within the normal boundaries of persuasion are especially great because nearly all terrorist acts create *negative* opinion rather than *favorable* opinion. It should be remembered, however, that the creation of such unfavorable opinion is sometimes a strategy designed to induce government reactions that will harm the public and generate even stronger negative opinion toward the government.

If one considers terrorist acts in accordance with traditional knowledge and theory of persuasion, one expects that short-term public opinion shifts will result from terrorist events. This can be of advantage to governments or terrorists, although history has shown that the crystallization of opinion has generally resulted in support for government efforts to halt terrorism. Because self-interest rather than other factors is most important in determining opinion, individuals' desires to survive and be free of the threat of terrorism would be expected to lead to strongly negative reactions to terrorism. Finally, because the public places great confidence in leaders during crises, such as terrorism campaigns, and because that confidence will be disturbed if leadership is not strong, loss of support for government can occur if government is unable to successfully cope with incidents of terrorism, to give the appearance that it is coping well, or to articulate and gain support for its policies.

S. E. Rada has noted the similarities between the work of terrorists and those in the public relations industry who work to persuade the public through the media:

> Modern terrorism and public relations share significant similarities. To a great extent, both are manufactured commodities owing their existence to the obsequiousness and pervasiveness of the electronic media. Both necessitate strategic planning, often trans-national in scope, sometimes involving large sums of money. Both invoke the power of symbolism. Both operate in open societies. And while they differ in tactics, one choosing coercion, the other persuasion, the end objective of influencing attitudes and behavior is the same.[6]

Terrorism is thus a unique form of persuasion: it does not employ the normal techniques of persuasion but relies more upon other communication elements as a means of achieving its goals.

During terrorist events and campaigns, nonstate perpetrators are not the only actors using persuasive techniques. Governments and social institutions being attacked use persuasive techniques to generate and solidify support for themselves and their policies and to gain public assent for actions against the perpetrators of the violent acts. Government spokespeople undertake these persuasive efforts by providing statements about the violence for news programs and appearing on current affairs shows. During these appearances, authorities downplay the perpetrators, their acts, and their motivations and emphasize the strength, effectiveness, and policies of officials.

Techniques often employed include refuting the statements of the perpetrators, diverting attention from issues raised by the terrorists to the violence itself and government responses to that violence, and minimizing the effectiveness of the acts and perpetrators.

Terrorism and Propaganda

Propaganda is a form of communication that attempts to persuade or manipulate opinions or actions of an individual or group toward political, religious, military, economic, or social ends. The manipulation is designed and carried out by other individuals or organizations through the use of expression or actions. The concept and term can be traced to 1622 when the Roman Catholic church established the *Congregatio de Propaganda Fide* (Congregation for Propagation of Faith) for the purpose of converting unbelievers, sponsoring missionaries, and spreading the gospel.[7]

Since that time, the techniques of propaganda have been widely used and refined in religious, political, social, and commercial arenas. Even when applied to only the political arena, the term *propaganda* is used with little agreement among scholars as to its meaning. That confusion is reflected among the public as well and exists even today. David Drescher has noted that "the term 'propaganda' conjures up images of governmentally inspired lies, often either in the context of a 'hot' or 'cold' war. Usually, Americans think of propaganda as an activity that is engaged in by authoritarian or totalitarian governments. In fact, propaganda may involve the truth, selective use of the truth, or outright fabrications."[8]

Agreement has been reached on three major characteristics of propaganda in recent years, however. Most scholars agree that it is *intentional* action, designed to *manipulate* audiences, and to induce *change* in thought or action. A key characteristic of propaganda is that the targets are not conscious of the attempted manipulation, and the public both as a mass and as single individuals within the mass are targeted. It is the deliberateness of this unconscious manipulation that separates propaganda from persuasion.

Propaganda has been found to be most effective when individuals are alone in the mass and when a group is psychologically fragmented and without group defenses against the messages. In such situations, propaganda is aimed at the individual and then ultimately integrated into the mass through individuals. The most effective method for doing this is through modern mass media. Audiences of such media are anonymous masses made up of individuals who do not know or have contact with the majority of other individuals in the audiences. This creates the conditions under which propaganda is most effective; presenting propaganda to large societies would not be possible without mass media.

In its broadest sense, propaganda includes (1) activities designed to modify opinions by employing psychological means to induce changes in attitudes and behavior; (2) psychological warfare, efforts made against an adversary in hopes of destroying morale or confidence in leaders; (3) reeducation and brainwashing, the use of psychological and educational techniques designed to change an adversary who is in physical custody into an ally; and (4) public relations and advertising, which attempt to adapt individuals to society, an organization, or a way of life by developing specific attitudes and beliefs.

Jacques Ellul goes further than most scholars when he argues that *all* forms of communication are propaganda. He maintains that propaganda is manifested in two major forms, integration propaganda and agitation propaganda. Integration propaganda is that intended to induce individuals to adjust their behavior or beliefs to a desired pattern, and agitation propaganda is that intended to lead individuals to some action, usually radical social action or rebellion. His paradigm clearly encompasses the specific types of propaganda actions described above.[9]

Under Ellul's paradigm, terrorist acts come under the heading of agitation propaganda, although most terrorist acts are not designed to agitate for a specific public action. Few terrorist acts and resultant media coverage are specifically designed to make the public embrace the cause of the terrorist. As a form of propaganda, however, terrorism is most like psychological warfare because it attempts to demoralize; to induce fear, anxiety, and lack of confidence in leadership; and to lead to instability in society that terrorists can further exploit for their purposes.

Media aspects of terrorism also contradict the basic characteristic of propaganda: that is, that such activity is unconscious manipulation. In incidents of terrorism, the public is well aware of the terrorists' desire to influence, and reaction to the violence is generally negative. Terrorists' use of violence, however, is rarely a direct attempt to immediately swing public opinion in their direction. Instead, terrorists rely upon the concept of the *propaganda of the deed*. That is, the terrorist act itself carries messages, and it is these messages that the perpetrators wish to propagate. Normally, these messages are that the nonstate terrorists are effective, that they must be taken seriously, that there is reason to fear them, that people are unhappy with the status quo, and that authorities are not in full control. Most actions classified as state terrorism rely upon propaganda of the deed to carry messages that public opposition to authorities will not be tolerated and that it is futile to resist the power of government.

Propaganda of the deed has its greatest effects when it involves major figures or significant carnage. The effectiveness of such acts is seen in the turmoil and public reaction that accompany assassinations of major figures, such as Anwar Sadat (killed October 6, 1981, by Moslem fundamentalists during a military parade) and Rajiv Gandhi (killed by a Tamil nationalist on May 21, 1991), or large-scale acts of terrorism that are so public and significant that they cannot be downplayed. Examples of the latter are the seizure and killing of Israeli athletes at the 1972 Olympic Games in Munich by the Palestinian group Black September, the seizure of the Grand Mosque at Mecca in Saudi Arabia in 1979 by fundamentalist Moslems that ended in the deaths of more than 150 persons, and the seizure of 300 hostages in the Colombian Palace of Justice by the April 19 Movement (M-19) with the subsequent killing of six judges including the head of the Colombian Supreme Court in November 1985. State terrorism is rarely limited to single acts; it usually involves prolonged campaigns of violence against civilians in which casualties rise and are perceived by the public over time.

One reason that the propaganda of the deed is so effective at carrying fear to the public is that terrorist violence strikes at basic human drives. The four major drives include self-preservation, satisfaction of hunger, security, and sex; acts of violence threaten two of these, thus heightening the sense of anxiety caused by incidents of terrorism.[10]

The propaganda of nonstate terrorist groups is usually not crafted to directly carry specific messages to the public as is most propaganda. Instead, the function of communicating more fully with the public is carried out by publicity, a form of communication in which media have a great role. But terrorist propaganda is often combined with such publicity to achieve its intentions.

Terrorism and Publicity

Publicity is an organized form of persuasion that attempts to influence opinion by focusing attention on causes, persons, or institutions. To those who wish to communicate with publics, it is one aspect of a communication program but not its totality. The main objective of publicity is to make something or someone known to the public.

Publicity is specifically designed to attract media attention that has been focused elsewhere. It normally seeks media interest to point out the good works or qualities of the subject and is crafted so the publicity reflects on the subject by creating an image of what it is and how it is important. The main function of publicity, however, is to raise public awareness. Terrorists have an advantage in gaining this type of publicity because the public and violent nature of their acts guarantees that media will provide some coverage. Many media organizations wish to carry the kind of information terrorist groups provide when that information helps explain why acts occurred. As a result, even small organizations can make themselves heard and known in a very short time. Walter Laqueur has noted that, in carrying out these efforts, "the media are the terrorist's best friend. The terrorist's act by itself is nothing; publicity is all."[11]

Although such media reports may serve terrorists' desires to have awareness of their actions, existence, and purposes raised, they do not guarantee favorable attention, support, or acceptance of causes or institutions by the public. Thus, one cannot immediately damn media for carrying information about terrorist groups. In fact, such media coverage can harm terrorists' purposes. Excessive publicity, for instance, can irritate the public and create false expectations that ultimately harm the overall purpose of communicating. Publicity of negative information is usually not sought by public relations practitioners, but it is clearly sought by terrorist groups, and its effect must differ from publicity of positive information.

Some critics of media coverage have argued that terrorists seek publicity for its own sake, not caring whether the news and its meaning is harmful as persuasive communication. This view equates terrorists to press agents who care only about media exposure, not about message content. It has been observed that such persons "don't care if the noteworthiness puts their clients or companies in a good light or a bad one. The important thing for them is to get the individual or company name into print or broadcast at all. These so-called 'publicity hounds' want attention at any cost."[12] Labeling perpetrators of terrorism as seekers of publicity for its own sake is simplistic and ignores very significant efforts by terrorists to direct news coverage both to present their cause in favorable ways and to disassociate them from acts that will bring significant negative responses to the cause.

In public relations, publicity campaigns are well planned, making clear identification of publics with whom awareness is desired, the images the campaign wishes to convey, and methods for achieving the goals of the campaign. Techniques for achieving goals normally include press releases, statements, articles for publications, and background information in the form of press kits, fact sheets, reference guides, news conferences, interviews, and visual materials.

Although some terrorist groups approach publicity with preplanning and an understanding of its impact, few groups make full use of the technique of publicity, and—contrary to popular opinion—not all groups are publicity seekers. (Terrorists who are publicity seekers, however, use most of the techniques normally employed by public relations professionals.) Some publicity campaigns by terrorists are planned, but experience has shown that much is unplanned or unanticipated.

Among terrorist groups, the larger and more organized groups employ more and highly sophisticated publicity techniques intent on portraying violent acts as rational and justified (Table 4.1). Smaller groups tend to have fewer direct contacts with media and use fewer publicity techniques. Some groups have official public relations apparatuses to present their views and promote their causes. The Palestine Liberation Organization, for example, has press offices in New York City and other major world capitals. The African National Congress maintains offices in a number of southern African nations and has spokespeople available in London and other European capitals. The Nicaraguan contras maintained press representatives in Washington, Miami, and Honduras; and the Mujahadeen of Afghanistan have offices in both the United States and Pakistan. The latter group was assisted in the mid-1980s by the Afghan Media Project, an educational program established by the CIA, funded by the United States Information Agency, and operated by Boston University, that taught press relations and journalistic techniques to the organization's representatives. The Irish Republican Army (IRA) is represented by Sinn Fein press offices in Belfast and Dublin.

Some terrorist groups, however, generally avoid the techniques of publicity, relying more heavily on the propaganda of the deed for awareness. Groups that eschew publicity often do so because they consider the media part of the enemy or are employing strict security measures. The Maoist Shining Path organization in Peru, for example, avoids media contact, shunning interviews and making only occasional statements about its activities. And some groups that use media for publicity limit

Table 4.1. Publicity techniques commonly employed by small and large terrorist groups

Technique	Small Groups	Large Groups
Press offices		x
Statements of responsibility	x	x
Multiple release points		x
Press releases		x
Multiple release points		x
Force publication of manifestos	x	
Audiovisual materials (videotapes, photos)	x	
News conferences		x
Interviews with group leaders	x	x
Press tours		x
Operate media		x
Large-scale propaganda of the deed	x	

that exposure. In Lebanon, both Hezbollah and Islamic Jihad, which make regular contact with media from various countries, have not made their hostages available for interviews or sought widespread and continuing publicity about them. At times, these groups have become so silent about the situation that the hostages have been dropped from the media agenda and the families of the hostages have themselves sought to elevate them to the media agenda again through pressure and activities designed to attract media coverage.

Sometimes publicity efforts are avoided to reduce pressure or counterterrorism against the perpetrators. This appears to have been the case in the bombing of Air India Flight 182, which crashed into the North Atlantic off Ireland in 1986, the bombing of Korean Airlines (KAL) Flight 858 on the Burmese border in 1987, and the bombing of Pan Am Flight 103 over Scotland in 1988. Responsibility for the attacks was never claimed, although Sikh separatists were implicated in placing a bomb aboard the Air India plane in Canada, a captured woman later confessed to being a North Korean agent and placing a bomb on the KAL aircraft, and Libyan officials were indicted for planning the Pan Am bombing.

When terrorist groups do seek publicity, it is necessary to consider the publics to which this publicity is directed. In doing so, the location and composition of the publics become important. One needs to understand *to whom* the terrorists are communicating and *why* in order to comprehend the purposes of the publicity effort. In some cases, publicity is aimed at domestic publics, individuals in the nation where the acts take place. In other situations, publicity is targeted to regional publics, individuals in nations surrounding the location of the acts, or to world publics, individuals in nations throughout the world or outside of the region in which the act occurred.

Specific publicity attempts can also single out specific audiences, and those publics must be identified to fully comprehend the nature of a publicity act. In some cases the publicity is aimed at colleagues in terrorism as a means of gaining the esteem of or showing solidarity with other terrorist groups, or it can be intended to boost the morale of those in the group committing the acts. In other cases publicity is aimed at sponsors of terrorist groups, those who support through financial and logistical aid, to show sponsoring individuals and nations that the perpetrators are effective and successful in carrying out their purposes and that the sponsors' support is well spent. In other cases, the intended audiences are government officials or the public at large.

The types of publicity generated also depend upon the nature of the violent act and at whom it was aimed. The duration of terrorist acts is important. Concise, brief incidents of violence receive the least publicity, usually lasting only a day or two. Ongoing incidents receive more publicity because they provide the opportunity for continuing coverage and for regional and world media representatives to reach the scenes. Prolonged incidents receive most publicity for the same reasons. The targets of terrorism also affect the amount of coverage. Attacks on low- and mid-level government officials receive less publicity than attacks on high officials, attacks on small numbers of civilians receive less publicity than attacks on large numbers of civilians, and attacks on citizens of a country receive more coverage within that country than do attacks on citizens of other countries.

Location of the terrorist act is an important publicity characteristic. Accessibility of the location to media correspondents and communication transmission facilities is necessary for large amounts of coverage. George Quester has pointed out that the takeover of the *Achille Lauro* cruise ship in 1985 was covered differently from aircraft hijackings and other terrorist incidents because of the lack of visibility of the ship and the action taking place. The inability of media to observe what happens aboard ships, such as the dumping of the body of Leon Klinghoffer off the *Achille Lauro* into the sea, reduces the impact of ships as a location for terrorist acts. "Since the ship will typically not come immediately dockside, the display of such evidence of a willingness to commit murder will always be more at a distance, and hence less seductive of media attention and world attention," Quester argues.[13]

Publicity clearly plays a part in most terrorist campaigns. The most commonly employed technique is a statement of responsibility for violent acts. Such statements are usually made in phone calls, letters, or tape recordings delivered to media in which terrorists claim responsibility for acts and provide a brief rationale for their behavior.

Such communiques often include distinctive *signatures* — symbols, phrases, or other identifying characteristics that provide some proof of identity and link the group to other activities. Elements of Islamic Jihad, which have been holding some U.S. hostages in Lebanon, have traditionally released statements in the city of Beirut; they are written in Arabic, and begin with the Koranic phrase, "In the name of Allah, the merciful, the compassionate." When a message purported to be from a group that has previously sent communiques to media arrives at news bureaus, many journalists look for such signatures as a means of verifying the message's origin.

In recent years, sophisticated terrorist organizations have also used such statements to apologize for actions. The Basque Homeland and Freedom (ETA) group, for instance, called a radio station in Madrid to apologize for the deaths of eighteen civilians and the injury of one hundred others in 1985 when a bomb destroyed a restaurant that was frequented by U.S. servicemen. The spokesman told the station that the bomb had gone off early and that the civilians were the unintended victims. "The bomb was meant as an attack against the Yankee armed forces. It was a mistake. We apologize to the victims," the caller said.[14] Similar apologies were issued by the Irish Republican Army after its bombing of Harrod's Department Store in London in 1983 that killed five persons and injured ninety and by the Irish National Liberation Army following the bombing of a parade review stand in Enniskillen, Northern Ireland, in November 1987 that killed eleven persons and injured nearly one hundred.

Occasionally, large manifestoes are produced and distributed along with claims of responsibility. This technique is usually limited to emergent organizations. In some instances, the publication of manifestoes has been required as a condition for the release of kidnapped individuals. This was often the case when business executives were seized in Europe and Latin America by communist terrorist groups during the 1960s and 1970s, but the tactic has been less used in recent years.

Another common publicity device is the provision of visual materials, most often in hostage situations. Photographs of victims and videotape of statements read by hostages are regularly provided by terrorist organizations to media to prove they hold the individuals and to carry their demands to the government or public. A particularly powerful use of videotape material occurred when the Syrian National Socialist Party released a videotaped interview with sixteen-year-old Sana Mheidleh, recorded just prior to her suicide bombing of an Israeli convoy in southern Lebanon in April 1985. In the tape she gave her reasons for the attack, apologized to her parents, and said she was about to become a martyr in the resistance to Israeli aggression.

News conferences with members of the press and representatives of terrorist groups are not uncommon. Clandestine news conferences are arranged in which journalists are taken to undisclosed locations to meet officials of terrorist groups. At times, news conferences featuring hostages have been held, but these are unusual. One such conference occurred when TWA Flight 847 was hijacked to Beirut in 1985 and five hostages were made available for interviews with journalists at Beirut International Airport. The news conference, which could be held openly because of the protection of the Amal militia and the inability of the government of Lebanon to control the country, became a near-fiasco as print photographers and television camera crews jumped on tables and pressed to get better shots of hostages. The situation got so out of hand that those holding the hostages removed them from the room and reorganized the room to provide added security and better vision for cameras before the interviews were finally held.

On some occasions, individual interviews with terrorist leaders have been held, usually on the same basis as clandestine news conferences or in locations where the individuals are provided protection by the government. Such was the case when NBC News correspondent Henry Champ interviewed Mohammad Abul Abbas, leader of the Palestine Liberation Front that was responsible for the hijacking of the *Achille Lauro*.[15] Champ declined to identify where the interview took place, citing restrictions agreed upon to gain the interview, but U.S. officials later identified the site as Algiers.

Press tours are often arranged in geographical areas that are controlled by terrorist groups or in which they openly operate. In recent years, the contras opposing the Sandinista government in Nicaragua, the Mujahadeen in Afghanistan, the Khmer Rouge in Kampuchea, and the Farabundo Marti National Liberation Front (FMLN) in El Salvador have provided such services to journalists.

News releases that cite developments in the organization's efforts and interpret events are provided by some terrorist groups, especially large, well-established groups with domestic and international support. Such groups also tend to be providers of background information in the form of press kits, fact sheets, reference guides, and so forth. These groups often have press offices or representatives to handle the preparation and distribution of such materials.

The level of media sophistication of groups engaged in violence should not be underestimated. Ray Nunn, the ABC News producer who directed coverage in Beirut of the hijacking of TWA Flight 847 in 1985, was questioned about the involvement of CIA director William Casey in the purchase of ABC by Capital Cities Communication. Nunn said that an Amal militiaman asked him, "Mr. Casey owns a lot of shares in your company, doesn't he?"[16] Howard Stringer of CBS News also recalled that "one of the first things we saw was the Amal [militia] sign in the Commodore Hotel telling us, 'All coverage is pool coverage.'"[17]

Similar media savvy was evidenced half a decade earlier in Tehran when American officials were held at the U.S. embassy. The captors and their supporters quickly learned how to effectively manipulate U.S. media by holding staged demonstrations and press conferences that were scheduled to coincide with satellite time, so they could reach the United States in time for nightly newscasts and ABC's "America Held Hostage," which later became "Nightline." Spokesmen for the hostage takers regularly made themselves available for interviews with local and national television and press reporters.[18]

It should also be noted that well-established and well-supported groups that employ terrorism often operate their own media to publicize their efforts among supporters and group members. For example, the Provisional Sinn Fein, the legal branch of the Provisional Irish Republican Army, publishes the newspaper *An Phoblacht,* which promotes the views of the group and provides its interpretation and reports of incidents in which the IRA is involved.[19] Similarly, the Palestine Liberation Organization operates the Voice of Palestine radio station, and its supporters operate several broadcasting and print media.

During the 1975 kidnapping of Peter Lorenz, the Christian Democratic candidate for mayor of West Berlin, by the Baader-Meinhoff organization, which later exchanged him for imprisoned colleagues, representatives of the terrorist group directed television coverage and broadcast times. A television journalist later noted, "We lost control of the medium. We shifted shows to meet their timetable. [They demanded that] our cameras be in a position to record each of the prisoners as they boarded a plane and our news coverage had to include prepared statements of their demands."[20]

One must be careful, however, not to interpret terrorists' media sophistication as preplanning. In the cases of the Iranian embassy takeover and the hijacking of TWA Flight 847, the perpetrators clearly had not anticipated the volume or extent of media interest and were not prepared to handle the demands of journalists in the early days of the events.

State terrorists rarely employ publicity techniques to garner media coverage of their activities. In most cases, governments do not wish to admit responsibility for such violence because it will result in a loss of legitimacy for authorities. As a result, press relations in such situations are usually limited to official denials of involvement or complicity in state terrorism. In cases where government involvement is clear and cannot credibly be denied, spokesmen and women will justify government acts by conveying disinformation about the victims of the violence and casting its violence as necessary, justified, and limited.

Summary

Many casual observers tend to overstate the value of propaganda and publicity of terrorism, citing it as one of the most important causes of terrorism. However, those who have studied it closely recognize that the impact of propaganda and publicity in all persuasive campaigns is limited without interpersonal communication to support its arguments. The negative aspects of terrorism clearly keep publicity from developing immediate support for the perpetrators or their views.

Propaganda and publicity are not without value for terrorists, however. They clearly serve an agenda-setting function by placing a conflict on the public's agenda and can lead to discussions of the issues that led to the terrorism. It should also be noted that when terrorist sources provide coverage of the events themselves or terrorist sources make statements and explain events, they do so to present themselves in the best light and thus employ words that intensify heroic and positive aspects of their causes and actions and downplay negative aspects. In addition, these groups sometimes attempt to manipulate the coverage through disinformation and misinformation. The Irish Republican Army, for instance, has at times misled the media by exaggerating police violence, altering the scenes of incidents to make police appear to have acted in an unprovoked fashion, and providing prepared witnesses that will relate events in a means that promotes their interests.[21]

Even if media carefully handle such information, the publicity generated by media messages about terrorist groups and actions tends to provide intense, dramatic coverage that develops sentiment to explore what is happening, extends public awareness of the organizations and their purpose, and spreads fear.

5

Government and News of Terrorism

GOVERNMENTS BECOME NEWSWORTHY in terrorist incidents when they or their citizens become victims of terrorism, or when they respond to acts of political violence against others, or when they engage in or support state terrorism. Both political and security officials interject themselves into the news when they publicly respond to an incident of violence or discuss the event with reporters.

The relationships between media and government and the problems of news coverage of terrorism differ depending upon whether nonstate or state terrorism is involved. This chapter explores the various relationships and problems that arise in covering the two major types of political terrorism and the influence upon and manipulation of coverage that can result.

News of Nonstate Terrorism

Because governments are a primary target of most nonstate terrorism, when incidents occur media place significant importance on the views of government officials, the effects of violence on governments, government policies toward terrorism, and the ability of governments to respond to and control such violence. This emphasis on governmental aspects surrounding terrorist incidents is compounded because it is often impossible for reporters to contact other sources or they are discouraged from doing so by government officials. It is usually impossible for reporters to discuss the incident with perpetrators or their supporters, and it is difficult for media to find terrorism specialists or political and social experts who are knowledgeable about an incident or its causes yet who are not affiliated with or have views similar to those of government officials.

When incidents of terrorism occur, governments targeted for the violence, governments of nations in which violence takes place, and nations whose citizens or flag vessels are victimized respond with an agenda of action that often includes the subtle manipulation of media to carry messages beneficial to the government. This occurs because officials usually have two overriding goals: (1) the short-term goal of ending the incident and saving or helping victims, and (2) the long-term goal of punishing the perpetrators and preventing further violence.

During terrorist incidents, governments attempt to control the immediate situation by reducing the initial confusion at the scene and putting into action strategies designed to end the incident in the most favorable way possible. For government officials, this generally means that the incident is rapidly ended, that there are no or few casualties among civilians or government security forces, and that the perpetrators appear to have failed in their efforts.

These governmental goals serve the purposes of showing the government's stability and strength and avoiding the appearance of impotence or of being at the mercy of perpetrators. Rapid conclusion of events of terrorism also reduces media coverage and thus reduces the opportunity for perpetrators to use the media as a platform or to have media investigate grievances that might have led to the violence.

When responding to incidents, governments can also either choose to take steps to inhibit the creation of future incidents by those involved or opt to take retaliatory measures. These goals can be served by a strong security response to an attack, resulting in the killing of perpetrators. In such a response, the price of terrorist acts to groups is deliberately made high so that strategists in the groups will reconsider their tactics and avoid similar acts in the future.

When either or both of these strategies are employed, the government uses its spokesmen and women and officials to convey messages about the event to perpetrators, the public, other governments, and potential terrorists. It does so by defining and explaining the events, the participants, and the potential significance of an act in a way that supports both public policy and any planned response. Government spokes-men use persuasive techniques to downplay the effectiveness and impact of terrorism and at times employ disinformation to mask their own violent activities or to promote public policy interests that might not be popular. These efforts often take the form of statements made in news conferences, interviews with reporters, and appearances on news and talk shows. The media, which depend significantly upon official spokes-men during incidents of terrorism, carry the government's views and thus create a perceptual reality within which most of the audience will view the violence.

The importance of violence in gaining media attention and the use of official personnel as the primary sources of information on political life and conflict have been noted by Stuart Hall and other observers. Civil servants, police personnel, and elected officials are the *primary defiers* of such activities and the most frequently quoted observers. *Secondary definers,* those who are not part of the governmental institu-tions and power structure, are allowed to comment on the events and portray their frame of reference much less frequently, if at all.[1]

Ronald Crelinsten argues that perpetrators of terrorism and govern-ment officials engage in a struggle to control access to media and media coverage surrounding acts of terrorism and that this struggle is similar to other situations where those in power struggle with social activists out-side the power structure.

> Whenever opposing discourses collide in the arena of political life, the media tends to favour the official discourse, which has easy, routinized access because it is legitimized by the power structure. Alternative dis-courses, and particularly radical or extremist ones, which are margin-alized and discredited by the power structure, penetrate the media only with difficulty and, when they do, tend to be treated in ways which marginalize and discredit them further. In time of crisis, however, the process of reproduction and reinforcement of the existing order can be disrupted by the successful penetration of alternative discourses into media to the extent that they hold their own with official attempts to discredit them.[2]

As a result, Crelinsten argues, terrorists attempt to attract media atten-tion to penetrate the media channels with their messages, and govern-ments attempt to discredit the messages through efforts to control cov-erage or define events in ways that support their views of the situation.

Officials make significant efforts to accomplish these goals by mak-ing themselves available to the media and providing comments upon the events. Official press relations with the media during terrorist incidents rarely are carried on by the principal government officials involved in dealing with the situation because they are directing efforts to acquire information, preparing response options, and directing operations. As a result, media duties fall to press spokesmen, agency heads or their subordinates, or other political personnel.

In order to prepare those who must deal with the press, the State Department has general media guidelines for terrorist incidents that stress government concerns about efforts to downplay terrorist propaganda and effectiveness, maintain stable relations with other governments involved, and protect operational security forces.[3] In addition, specific guidance materials are usually prepared by the interagency situation team at the State Department during each major incident for appropriate agencies and spokesmen. Those dealing with the press rarely have direct involvement in or understanding of the government response and are sometimes specifically given false information so they can manipulate media or convey misleading information with a sincerity not possible if they were forced to deliberately mislead. Other members of the power structure, particularly political officials, make themselves available for comment about terrorist incidents with little of the prompting or advice given official spokesmen. Nevertheless, their views tend to support the official pronouncements and views of the government as a whole due to their positions in the power structure.

Military authorities are also concerned about the issue of press coverage and have their own guidelines for dealing with the media during incidents in which military installations or personnel are targeted or in which military personnel take part in security operations. Among these plans are the briefing of military commanders, spokesmen, and military victims about how to deal with the press, topics to be discussed, and information that should be withheld from media. U.S. Navy Capt. Brent Baker, writing in *Military Media Review,* says it is the duty of a public affairs officer (PAO) to

> brief not only the media but his commander, members of a rescue force, former hostages and hostages' next of kin before they are exposed to the news media interview or news conference.
>
> In these pre-media briefs the PAO should tell concerned personnel and relatives the questions to expect from the news media, including guidance on what they can and cannot comment upon.[4]

In addition to struggling to control how terrorist acts and perpetrators are depicted, officials use the media to carry a variety of messages to the perpetrators of terrorism, the public, and potential terrorists during such events. These messages have both general and specific purposes related to the maintenance of the existing order and the resolution of the existing incident. Some are specifically prepared by the operational staff, but most are standard messages based on policy and traditional government views and responses.

MESSAGES TO PERPETRATORS. In nearly every incident, government spokesmen and women attempt to send general messages to those perpetrating the violence and other members and supporters of the group involved. These communications are designed to publicly counter the destabilizing goals of terrorism.

The most common themes in these messages are that the government is not afraid of the perpetrators; that the act is more of a nuisance than a threat; that the government, rather than the perpetrators, remains in control of the incident; and that the perpetrators will not get away with the act. In many incidents, officials convey to the perpetrators the idea that they should not make the situation worse by killing or injuring any hostages under their control or extending the scope of the violence.

In some cases, governments employ the media to convey more specific communications to perpetrators. At times, authorities not wishing to directly communicate threatening information through negotiators might use media channels for such information. The information might be explicit — such as a direct threat of retaliation against supporters of the perpetrators or prisoners held by the government if hostages are harmed — or implicit — such as threats contained in release of information about new weapons or security or military units being moved to the scene of an ongoing incident or a region in which acts of terrorism have been occurring.

In some cases, when other channels are not available or governments or perpetrators refuse to deal directly with each other, media channels are used by both sides to send messages to each other through the mediation of journalists. This is a form of media diplomacy. Media personnel, for example, might interview a government official who, for policy, protocol, or other reasons, cannot or will not speak directly with representatives of a government sympathetic to a terrorist group or a representative of the group itself. Immediately after that interview, they might turn to the other party for reaction and comment. In some cases, the two might speak directly to or respond to each other in the format of a current affairs interview show when they would not do so otherwise, and these exchanges of ideas and opinions can be helpful in leading to resolution of prolonged events.

MESSAGES TO THE PUBLIC. When they are targets of terrorism, governments regularly use media channels to communicate with the citizens of their nations to convey the "evil" of their opponents who are engaging in the violence and to assert the stability and control of the government over the situation.

A major goal of a government is to portray political violence against itself and its allies as criminal, uncivilized, and lunatic. The perpetrators are purported to be without justification for their actions. Such portrayals can help create a climate of opinion against the initiators of the violence that permits wider latitude for government response. Governments worldwide attack political violence by defining it as uncivilized and illegal. In El Salvador, for example, after human rights official Rene Joaquin Cardenas was shot and killed in December 1987, the head of the government human rights office called the killing "a cowardly and criminal act."[5] A similar characterization was made by Egyptian Foreign Minister Boutros Ghali after gunmen — believed to be Israeli — stormed the home of PLO leader Khald al-Wazir in Tunis and assassinated him in April 1988. "We vehemently condemn and regard with extreme shock and repugnance this criminal action against the PLO leadership," the official said.[6] U.S. government officials responding to the Kuwait Airways' hijacking in April 1988 used similar rhetoric. "The hijackers are murderers trying to free other convicted murderers," said Charles Redman, spokesman for the State Department. "They must be punished. We would expect any country which has the opportunity to prosecute them for their crimes."[7] After a truck exploded in a vegetable market in Tripoli, Lebanon, that same month, killing nearly five dozen persons, that nation's acting prime minister, Salim Hoss, called the attack a "barbaric atrocity" and said "all hands must team up to stop these executioners from committing further crimes."[8]

Governments also try to frame events in a context that supports their own views and policies. For example, the Reagan administration attempted for most of its tenure to place the sole blame for international terrorism on the Soviet Union, Libya, Syria, and Nicaragua, regularly employing rhetoric to that effect when an attack took place. Similarly, an Israeli government spokesman publicly attempted to classify all members of the Palestine Liberation Organization as one group, making no distinction between the factions led by Abul Abbas and Yasser Arafat, yet the Israeli government privately makes these distinctions and has had unofficial meetings with the moderate factions. After the attacks on the Rome and Vienna airports in December 1985, Israeli officials differed significantly from U.S. officials on which governments provided the support for those responsible for the attacks. The Israelis pointed the finger at Syria, an immediate security threat. The U.S. officials chose to blame Libya because doing so supported their views and public policies in the Middle East, especially since Syria had been more open to discussion and negotiations involving incidents in Lebanon at that time.

Efforts to portray events by government officials are sometimes contradictory due to differing interests of political and career government servants and individuals from different branches or agencies of government. These interests can keep agencies from coming to full agreement on what constitutes terrorism, how terrorists should be handled, how incidents should be interpreted, and what messages should be conveyed to and through media.

The problem was starkly illustrated when the car bombing attack, in which 250 servicemen died, was made on the U.S. Marines' barracks in Beirut in 1983. Many political critics in Congress argued that the attack revealed the bankruptcy of U.S. policy in Lebanon and the failure of the administration to articulate and carry out a coherent policy for the use of military forces. Administration figures in the White House labeled the event as terrorism and thus framed the event in a way that allowed them to ignore addressing the policy issues. Some officials in the Defense and State Departments disagreed with the view that the attack constituted terrorism and preferred to view it as an act of war or low-intensity conflict. Indeed, Defense Department officials recommended disciplinary action against military officers for not better protecting the troops in a war zone, thus transferring some responsibility for the attack to the government itself. The White House rejected any public discipline, however, and the military acquiesced to laying the responsibility for the deaths on terrorism rather than admitting negligence that would be politically damaging.

In addition to framing events in a context that supports government views and policies, governments respond to events with an attempt to appear stable and in control despite terrorism. If their response is carried in the media, as it normally is, it gives the appearance that the government is able to cope with the situation and that it has more information than it might in fact possess. It is not surprising that governments should take such a stance, since one goal of terrorism is to undermine a government's credibility and stability.

MESSAGES TO POTENTIAL TERRORISTS. Governments also use media channels carrying news about political violence to deter potential terrorists or groups that sometimes engage in terrorism but are not currently doing so. Through rhetoric of strength, diminishing the accomplishments of those who use violence, parading sophisticated weapons, discussing training of counterterrorist groups, or releasing intelligence information, governments warn potential terrorists that their acts will be more dangerous than previously expected or that the government is able to cope with such events.

Government spokesmen and women regularly assert that they will never negotiate with terrorists or provide rewards for violent acts. Yet they regularly negotiate during incidents and provide rewards, although these negotiations are often carried out through "back channels" or the rewards are given to supporters rather than to the group itself.

Such, of course, was the case when figures in the Reagan administration traded weapons and supplies to Iran as a means of getting groups in Lebanon to release U.S. hostages, a move that led to the Iran-contra scandal when income from the transactions was diverted to the Central American conflict. Even the government of Israel, which is publicly lauded for its nonnegotiation policies, has regularly negotiated with Palestinian and Arab paramilitary groups that have captured Israeli military personnel, and it has released Palestinian and Arab prisoners as part of those negotiations.

Government-Media Conflicts about News

In Western liberal democratic nations, government officials tend to disagree with media personnel about the uses that should be made of available information and about their separate roles in society. These types of disagreements bring them into regular conflict during the best of times, and the conflict is intensified during incidents of terrorism. These problems occur because Western news media accept a position as the "fourth estate" of nations and see their role as one of an overseer of the activities of state.

In addition, the two differ significantly in terms of their relationships to information. The primary function of media is to collect and disseminate information. When government handles information, however, its bureaucracies work to collect, save, and use information as a means of power. Often this means that the possession of information that others do not have brings additional power or influence. In these situations, media employees work vigorously to gain access to such information. During terrorist events, the separate approaches clash significantly and officials worry that information might provide additional power to the perpetrators or threaten the safety of victims. The position taken by officials is not unrealistic. Many officials would be delighted if media carried no news at all about terrorist incidents. Because that type of control is not possible in liberal democratic states, however, they settle on using media and manipulating coverage to produce more desirable results for their purposes.

The difficulties posed by the different approaches to information and the adversarial relationship between media and government are manifested in a variety of coverage issues, including (1) protecting sensitive information, (2) interfering with government operations, (3) conferring status on perpetrators of terrorism, (4) contributing to the spread of terrorism, and (5) contributing to the development of fear among the populace.

PROTECTING SENSITIVE INFORMATION. Government spokesmen and women have regularly criticized media for releasing information that might endanger individuals held by terrorists. The criticism arose to prominence in the 1970s after several significant errors in judgment by media resulted in sensitive information reaching terrorists when it was reported by media personnel. A major concern of officials is that information about the identities of hostages or kidnap victims, which might indicate a greater worth for those persons in negotiations or otherwise jeopardize their safety because of their occupations, might reach the perpetrators if reported by media. The type of information that might be sensitive varies from incident to incident, depending upon the perpetrators, their attitudes and values, and the rationale for their actions. Types of sensitive identity information that regularly raise concerns in this regard are citizenship, ethnic background, religion, and government employment.

An example of such information being released during a hijacking occurred when Leah Abramson called the *Miami Herald* to see if her nephew, Michael Brown, was on the hijacked plane. A reporter confirmed that Brown was on the plane, and Abramson and the journalist discussed reports that the hijackers were attempting to identify Jewish passengers. The paper later printed Abramson's response that "I'm praying. . . . We're Jewish but Michael doesn't look Jewish, thank God. I just hope they don't hurt him. That's what worries me. Thank God, in this country we don't have to put religion on our passports."[9] Wire services then used the quote in their dispatches and it was carried in other publications, including the *Washington Post*. Although Brown was not singled out as a result of the coverage, it carried with it the potential for harm and underscores the concerns of authorities about the information carried by media.

Government officials who have worked with media to protect sensitive information have found that reporters will voluntarily withhold vital information or acquiesce to government requests if good reasons exist. An example of this cooperation occurred during the hijacking of TWA Flight 847 when U.S. television networks and print journalists knew that three government employees on the plane had top security clearances and one was a National Security Agency employee. The media withheld the news so as not to jeopardize their safety and national security interests.

Another example of this cooperation occurred when William Buckley, the first secretary of the political section of the U.S. embassy, was kidnapped in Beirut in March 1985 by Islamic Jihad. U.S. media reported his kidnapping and the job title, but withheld news that Buckley was actually the CIA station chief. Although they possessed the sensitive information, no U.S. media published or broadcast it for a year until it was determined that Buckley had died as a result of injuries sustained during torture and interrogation.

Another example of withholding information of interest to government occurred when Lt. Col. William R. Higgins, commander of the United Nations Truce Supervising Organization, was kidnapped in Lebanon in February 1988 by a group calling itself the Organization of the Oppressed of the Earth. Most major media organizations knew he had been an important aide to former Secretary of Defense Caspar Weinberger and withheld that information until the Voice of Lebanon radio broadcast the news and the views of the Hezbollah organization that Higgins was an intelligence agent.

Journalists are willing to withhold sensitive information during terrorist events when they understand its significance. In instances where government explains desires for secrecy during events, it is usually offered. Problems appear to occur most when journalists do not realize the significance of specific information or its potential for harm and are left to exercise their own judgment. This problem is apparently compounded because officials appear to offer little guidance in these matters or only ask that certain information be withheld when government employees are involved.

INTERFERING WITH GOVERNMENT OPERATIONS. Security forces have criticized coverage of military and police responses to terrorism, especially during ongoing events, when media attention has revealed deployment of personnel and weapons, strategies, and other information that might endanger personnel or the effectiveness of these responses. Media have not been criticized for deliberately providing such information to perpetrators, but instances have occurred in which such information has reached terrorists because of inadvertent release caused by the lack of care or the lack of understanding about the nature of information.

M. Cherif Bassiouni has underscored the difficulties caused by releasing information that can be dangerous to authorities and argues that some information should be withheld, including information "about police tactics, negotiating strategies, or apparent sincerity or lack thereof in dealing with terrorists. The release of such information only endangers lives without contributing to the public good."[10]

Of particular concern to many security officials is live broadcasting of television pictures and radio news from the site of terrorist incidents. The use of the visual images and information for intelligence gathering on what officials are doing has resulted in serious problems in a number of situations. In the mid 1970s, for example, after a British Airways flight en route to Libya was seized by hijackers who demanded the release of prisoners being held by Egypt, authorities attempted to mislead the hijackers into releasing hostages by landing another plane on which the freed prisoners were supposed to be traveling. A reporter broadcast information about the ruse, and the hijackers killed a passenger as a result.[11] In October 1977, another example of interference occurred during the hijacking of a Lufthansa airliner, when a radio reporter broadcast the news that the pilot of the aircraft was providing information to authorities by concealing it in messages between the pilot and authorities. The hijackers, who were monitoring radio reports, heard the news report and killed the pilot.[12]

More recently, media were severely criticized for revealing the movement of Delta Force, the U.S. counterterrorist unit, to the Middle East in preparation for a rescue attempt during the hijacking of TWA Flight 847 in 1985. Government officials and media critics argued that as a result of the news reports the hostages were moved from a location from which they could have been rescued and that the media had thus harmed government efforts.

Although the incident illustrates how sensitive information can be used by terrorists, it must be noted that the television networks received the information from Pentagon sources. NBC News employees, for example, were summoned to the Pentagon to be briefed on the movement of the troops and were not told to withhold the information. Producer Ray Nunn, who was running the network's news operation in Beirut, called the network headquarters from Lebanon to confirm that the Defense Department wanted the Delta Force movement reported before he put it on the air in a broadcast from Beirut. He was assured that the government, in fact, wanted the information carried as a means of bringing pressure on the hijackers.

Other media efforts to cover government operations during the hijacking incident raise concern about potential interference and harm. During the two-week ordeal, ABC News chartered an airplane to fly over the U.S. Sixth Fleet in the Mediterranean Sea in order to observe and report the movements and activities of Marines and special forces that might be aboard. Such information could have led to operational problems for the military if troops had been dispatched on a rescue or retaliation mission before the hijacking was ended through negotiations.

During the later hijacking of the *Achille Lauro*, the terrorists placed Western hostages on deck and warned that they would be harmed if any aircrafts or ships approached the vessel. Military authorities, worried that media might charter aircraft to fly near the ship to obtain photographs and videotapes, with the possible result of violence against the hostages or a complication of efforts to resolve the incident, requested media not to approach the ship. News organizations complied, so there is clearly room for cooperation if military and press organizations deal effectively with each other.

CONFERRING STATUS ON TERRORISTS. Many government officials argue that media coverage is damaging because it confers status on those who commit acts of violence and legitimizes their causes and actions. Most authorities express particular concern when press attention is focused on small terrorist organizations or factions or the leaders of groups with little social importance. Others, however, damn coverage of all groups and persons engaging in political violence, even groups with supporters numbering in the hundreds of thousands.

The idea that media confer status on those they focus upon has been well described by Lazarsfeld and Merton, who maintain that "the mass media bestow prestige and enhance the authority of individuals and groups by legitimizing their status. Recognition by the press, radio or newsreels testifies that one has 'arrived,' that one is important enough to have been singled out from the large anonymous masses, that one's behavior and opinions are significant enough to demand the public's notice."[13]

Gabriel Weimann applies this idea to terrorism, noting that press attention enhances "the status of the people, problem, or cause behind a terrorist event. Terrorists' success in attracting media attention may then guarantee worldwide awareness and recognition of the political, racial, or religious problem that caused the event."[14]

Concern over the great amount of coverage surrounding the hijacking of TWA Flight 847 and the extensive responses given by U.S. officials to efforts of various parties involved in the negotiations resulted in the State Department placing a ban on government officials appearing on morning talk shows. This was done to try to reduce coverage and the legitimacy that coverage was supposedly giving the demands of the hijackers and various negotiators, notably Nabih Berri.

The idea that media coverage can give status to perpetrators of political violence and their causes is not without basis. In fact, an experimental study of terrorism coverage found that when audiences were not directly affected by the acts of violence and no significant preexisting attitudes were present, reports about the incidents resulted in audiences slightly improving their images of the perpetrators and giving status to the causes promoted by those engaging in violence. The research found that "changes toward positive evaluations are correlated with a moderate level of objection to terrorism. . . . Those respondents with moderate objections to terrorism tended to change their evaluations after being exposed to the press clippings, while those with extreme objections tended to hold to the image they had had before reading them."[15]

Another study of public attitudes toward terrorism and terrorists explored how a television audience was affected by viewing an NBC News special documentary about the seizure of the Achille Lauro and U.S. actions to capture the perpetrators. The before-and-after study found no evidence that watching the program caused the audience to view the terrorists more sympathetically or that the terrorists' cause was legitimized.[16]

Thus, in situations where attitudes already exist, the results reinforce existing views. This result was also found in studies of U.S. television and print coverage of the Irish Republican Army, the Red Brigades, and the Fuerzas Armadas de Liberacion Nacional (FALN). These studies found that the coverage was dominated by government positions and reinforced negative government attitudes toward the groups, thus mobilizing public opinion toward strong counterterrorism measures.[17] Another study of terrorists and their actions found that strongly negative characterizations of them by government officials were regularly carried by media, another evidence that media reports convey the predominant views of authorities.[18]

Governments make significant efforts to halt direct communication by individuals or groups engaging in terrorism in order to help reduce legitimization that might occur. Pressures are regularly brought to bear against news organizations that have interviewed perpetrators, and some nations outlaw such interviews altogether. Authorities try to limit access to audiences so that perpetrators cannot convey in their own words the meaning of the events taking place and perhaps sway some viewers, listeners, or readers to believe the action or cause is justified.

Although there might be reason to ask media not to carry interviews during incidents of terrorism so that no direct reward for the violence underway is provided, denying access at other times is often merely a power maintenance function of government efforts to deny any voice to opponents. This was clearly the case in 1985 when the British Broadcasting Corporation was forbidden to broadcast the documentary "Real Lives: At the Edge of the Union" about terrorism in Northern Ireland. Officials in the government of Margaret Thatcher were angered because the documentary contained an interview with Martin McGuinness, an elected member of the Ulster Assembly and a spokesman for Sinn Fein — the public and legal organization representing interests of the Irish Republican Army. McGuinness's interview disturbed authorities because he attempted to justify the IRA opposition to British rule and to treatment of Catholics by Protestants. Home Secretary Leon Brittan said the airing of the program would be "wholly contrary to the public interest."[19]

When NBC News, in May 1986, broadcast a three-and-a-half minute interview with Abul Abbas, head of the Palestine Liberation Front, whose members hijacked the ship *Achille Lauro* six months prior, the news organization was subjected to swift and pointed criticism. "Terrorism thrives on this kind of publicity," charged State Department spokesman Charles Redman. He said it "encourages the terrorist activities we're all seeking to deter."[20]

SPREADING TERRORISM. Officials argue that such interviews and widespread coverage of acts of terrorism lead to the spread of terrorism, encouraging groups and individuals who might not otherwise engage in violence to do so and encouraging other groups to increase the scale of their violence to gain coverage. At the American Bar Association meeting in London in 1985, Prime Minister Margaret Thatcher told the gathered attorneys that democracies "must find a way to starve the terrorists and hijackers of the oxygen of publicity on which they depend."[21] The efforts to induce self-restraints or impose government restraints on the media stem from the belief that coverage of terrorism and terrorists creates more terrorism and terrorists, or at least may encourage some terrorists to engage in some spectacular violence to gain more coverage.

The idea that terrorism would not occur or spread without media coverage has been widely heralded by counterterrorism advisors and researchers who have been unable to significantly control or end terrorism through other efforts. This media contagion argument has been repeatedly used to justify efforts to alter media coverage by those who are willing to sacrifice some basic freedoms in hope of keeping society safe.

This has occurred despite the fact that there is no significant scientific evidence that media coverage promotes such acts of violence. During the past two decades, the literature associating media with terrorism and implicating media as a contagion of such violence has grown rapidly. When one carefully dissects that literature, however, one finds no credible evidence that media are an important factor in inducing and diffusing terrorist acts. Most books, articles, essays, and speeches on the subject are composed of sweeping generalities, conjecture, supposition, anecdotal evidence based on dubious correlations, and repetition of weak arguments and nonscientific evidence offered by other writers on the subject.[22]

When one carefully examines what has been written about terrorism and media, and the negligible research on the topic, it becomes clear that there is no credible evidence that media are an important factor in inducing or diffusing terrorist acts, that there is no evidence that media are a necessary and sufficient condition for terrorism to exist, and that no study based on accepted research methods has established a cause-and-effect relationship between media coverage and the spread of terrorism or even a significant correlation between coverage and the spread of terrorism. Nevertheless, public officials and some scholars—and even editors, reporters, and columnists—continually link the two elements and present the relationship as proven, ignoring other equally important arguments that coverage might actually reduce the level and scope of violence.

Rudolf Levy, a Defense Department expert on terrorism who has taught at the U.S. Army Intelligence Center and School, recently conveyed the media-as-contagion view to the military community in the publication *Military Intelligence,* saying that coverage has the effect of "encouraging the formation of new groups . . . keeping the terrorist's organization's name before the public and 'the masses' on whose behalf the terrorists supposedly act, leading other less successful groups or individuals to commit more daring acts of terrorist violence [and] tempting terrorists, who have received favorable media coverage in the past, to attempt to seize control of the media."[23] A similar view was expressed by the American Legal Foundation, a right-wing group that recently argued that the government should restrict media coverage. In a book published by the foundation, the group argues that "because they give the terrorists a convenient stage to vent their political grievances, the media actually encourage terrorism and may promote the increasing violence and drama of terrorist attacks."[24]

Members of the media have also considered and, presumably, unwittingly promoted the contagion idea, as well as the more plausible idea that some kinds of coverage can result in some terrorist actions under some circumstances. This latter view is more sophisticated than the simple coverage-causes-terrorism view and recognizes that there is a symbiotic relationship between terrorism and coverage. Although they recognize that media might have some effect on those predisposed to political violence, journalists tend to more strongly support the idea that society is best served if citizens have full knowledge of the ideas and events—even terrorist ideas and events—occurring around them.

NBC News President Larry Grossman, who defends his network's decision to air the Abbas interview, dealt with the issue of media and terrorism during the Society of Professional Journalists/Sigma Delta Chi (SPJ/SDX) regional meeting in Columbus, Ohio, in the spring of 1986: "Does television allow itself to be 'used' by terrorists and does television coverage therefore encourage terrorist acts? The answer is yes to both," he said. "The very existence of television undoubtedly bears some responsibility for the 'copycat' syndrome of terrorism today."[25] Although such concern about the impact of coverage is evidence of sensitivity to government concerns by journalists, it conveys the overly broad and unsubstantiated generalizations about the power of media coverage.

Some of the most serious terrorism researchers are not convinced that media can be blamed for causing or assisting terrorism, and many do not advocate external controls. Studies by the CIA and by independent scholars who have considered why terrorism spreads reveal a variety of important factors but do not lay the blame on media. Instead, they reveal the most important factors to be terrorist groups helping each other, state sponsorship of terrorism, poor security measures by authorities, and rapid international transportation.

While the work of these researchers has not specifically studied the contagion effect of media coverage per se, their related contagion studies are important. The most significant research has been conducted by Midlarsky, Crenshaw, and Yoshida, who sought to answer the question of why terroristic acts spread across nations in western Europe and Latin America. Using the theory of hierarchy, the researchers attempted to explain the spread of terrorism among nations. In the case of western

Europe, the researchers found that "terrorism spreads from the least powerful to the most powerful, from the weak states to the strong."[26] That study found that European terrorist groups, for example, borrowed ideology, rhetoric, and methods from the Third World. The biggest contagion effect was found in the transfers of the technique of bombing in both Latin America and Europe, with kidnappings most significant in Latin America and hijacking to a lesser extent there. Media were never mentioned as a cause of the diffusion of terrorist techniques.

Security adviser Edward Heyman and CIA researcher Edward Mickolus later disputed the full findings of the Midlarsky study, citing inadequacies in its data base and some of its inferences, but they did not dispute its general concept. The two argued that their own research indicated that two noncontagion diffusion factors were important in spreading the violence: extensive intergroup cooperation and the idea of transporting terrorist acts to locations where they could best be carried out. They argued that transportation was the biggest factor.[27] Again, no mention of media coverage was made as an important cause of the spread of terrorism.

Brian Jenkins, who directs the Rand Corporation's terrorism research project and appears frequently on network TV discussions of terrorism, says the news media "are responsible for terrorism to about the same extent that commercial aviation is responsible for airline hijackings." He argues that "the vast communications network that make up the news media are simply another vulnerability in a technologically advanced and free society."[28]

Studies by the Rand Corporation have found some evidence of contagion in the diffusion process of terrorist activity types. Jenkins, although unwilling to damn news coverage as the culprit, has noted clusters of occurrences in airline hijackings and embassy sieges and indicated media *might* have played a role in those occurrences.[29] Other research on terrorism has noted that in the case of many airline hijackings since the 1970s, for example, terrorist hijackers often had specific knowledge of radio, navigation, and operating equipment on aircraft and of commercial aviation practices, suggesting that they had specialized training and that extensive planning of campaigns of hijacking had occurred. These factors tend to indicate that some of the clusters of hijackings were planned well in advance and should not be blamed on media coverage of the events alone.

SPREADING FEAR.   Officials regularly criticize the style of media coverage, arguing that coverage that emphasizes threat and violence evokes the fear-and-terror response that perpetrators of such acts wish to exploit in audiences. Franco Salomone has argued that "probably the most significant question for the media . . . is the issue of *sensationalism*."[30]

The inherent sensationalism of broadcast coverage—especially the drama of immediacy and photography of carnage—makes almost any coverage of terrorism by television and radio sensational. The development of the technology of television brought about instantaneous world communication that makes possible live television coverage throughout most events, and this brings the incident "closer" to the world of the audience as well.[31]

Television has a unique advantage over other media in that dramatic live news events are what the medium, by its nature, is best suited to cover. In the case of terrorist incidents, something has happened that can be depicted by the images projected onto the television screen. When there is time for cameras to reach the scene before the incident is concluded, as is often the case in hostage takings and hijackings, television is provided the opportunity to use the inherent sensational drama of these events in its coverage. In ongoing terrorist incidents, television cameras usually focus on police and military units and their unusual weapons and vehicles because the newspeople are not able to establish direct contact with perpetrators themselves. Such events are made for television in that they are good drama with which the public can satisfy morbid curiosity.

When television covers incidents such as bombings and attacks on civilians, news crews usually get to the scene after the fact and focus only on the spectacle of the incident, whether the spectacle is wreckage, bodies, blood, or weapons. The result is also inherently sensational. Much sensationalism results from the newsbreak, special reports, and program formats of television that give greater import to terrorist events than they might deserve. Sensationalism is heightened by news "teasers" that advertise developments that will be covered on newscasts by presenting exceptionally brief updates that are intended to heighten drama and induce the viewer to watch further.

The problems of television coverage can be magnified if a commercialized, tabloid approach is employed in addressing the issue of terrorism. This is starkly illustrated by the May 1989 "American Expose" special hosted by Jack Anderson. The two-hour program called "Target: USA!" explored international terrorism with graphic, sensationalized reporting and featured simulations, recreations, and actual footage of acts of terrorism. The set from which Anderson hosted the program was an American flag, covered with a bull's eye target, and overlaid with photographs of Moammar Khadafy and Ayatollah Khomeini. The program title—"Target: USA!"—was created as a bullet riddled graphic that was electronically placed throughout the program. The effect of the visuals, the tone of the report, and the language used was to heighten viewers' fear and probably did as much to serve that purpose as the acts of violence on which the program reported.

Print coverage can be equally sensational through the use of headlines and photographs, illustrations, and language employed. Screaming 48- and 60-point headlines using active and inflammatory words to attract attention and sell the story to readers are common. Headlines such as "Bomb Rips Bar; Kills 15" or "Hijackers Threaten Hostage Deaths" are often accompanied by evocative photographs that emphasize the sensational aspects of an incident.

Even when print media attempt to put events into perspective, something better suited to newspapers and magazines than television due to their formats and reader expectations, headlines and illustrations often emphasize sensational aspects. For example, when Associated Press writer Charles Hanley produced a five-part series in April 1986 about the problem and causes of terrorism, it was sent to subscribers with a graphic design for the series by Cynthia Geer that portrayed a sinister, Arabic-appearing man holding an automatic weapon and the words "Target: Terror." When the *St. Petersburg Times,* one of the nation's most respected medium-sized papers, ran articles about terrorism, it used a highly inflammatory and sensational logo of a hooded individual holding an automatic weapon surrounded by the words "Terrorists. They Will Come" to illustrate each article in the series.

Partially because of the media's sensational approach, and the lack of context, historical understanding, and grasp of the political and social issues involved, members of the media make a terrorist situation difficult for the public to understand. As a result, the public can come to overestimate the frequency of terrorism and its import on the flow of world events. A form of siege mentality brought on by fear can develop, and that fear can spread throughout the populace.

In the United States, for example, thousands of tourists changed travel plans to southern Europe and the Mediterranean after the three major terrorist incidents that occurred there in 1985. The manner in which these incidents were reported presumably colored potential tourists' views of the area. Princess Cruise Lines was forced to cancel a cruise in the Mediterranean after the *Achille Lauro* incident because of cancellations and reduced bookings. After the attacks on the Rome and Vienna airports, TWA lost at least 4,000 reservations for flights to southern Europe, and tourism officials projected a 50 percent loss in tourism from the United States for 1986.

Fear, however, is not spread only by news reports about acts of terrorism. Government officials can also spread that fear through their statements about terrorism. In 1982, for instance, U.S. authorities raised great fear through public announcements that it had intelligence data that proved that Libyan "hit squads" were in and were coming to the United States. Discussions of the threat and efforts by State Department, Defense Department, and law enforcement officials to respond to the terrorists on talk shows and newscasts became a major topic of discussion on the public agenda. In 1985 and 1986, intelligence agencies and law enforcement officials issued public alerts to news media that attacks were expected at specific U.S. airports. In 1990, as allied forces prepared for war against Iraq, officials issued public warnings about travel dangers in the Middle East and Mediterranean posed by terrorists. The alerts were issued as a means of helping local police forces increase security when intelligence reports, threatening phone calls, and terrorism elsewhere suggested threat of terrorism at the airports. In one case, the U.S. media widely heralded government alerts for an attack on a U.S.-bound aircraft from Canada after officials in that nation increased security following an informant's warning of an impending attack. News of the alert was carried for more than a week before authorities determined the informant had perpetrated a hoax. Nonetheless, the public had been terrorized by the incident. Although such alerts potentially aided local police, making them public provided those who engaged in terrorism a victory without any risks because the public became fearful and the attacks might not even have been planned in the first place.

News of State Terrorism

When governments engage in terrorism, the efforts often include actions designed to inhibit news coverage or specific efforts to direct coverage so that it does not cover government-sponsored violence as terrorism. It has been observed that "it may be more advantageous at times for terrorism from above (state sponsored) to reduce media exposure of repressive violence. . . . In the case of serious state-sponsored violations of human rights—such as the use of torture, and arbitrary arrests and detentions—the state may well use all of its powers to prevent dissemination of such news."[32]

Efforts to prevent discussion of government violence regularly result in attacks on journalists and news organizations by military and security forces and paramilitary groups linked to governments. Efforts to keep state terrorism out of the news have resulted in the use of torture, arrest, and deaths of journalists. In 1987, for example, at least twenty-five journalists were killed worldwide and ten more were kidnapped or disappeared without a trace.[33] Those deaths resulted from about eight hundred separate attacks on journalists throughout the world during the year.[34] Many of the journalists were victims of state terrorism or state-supported terrorism as elites attempted to maintain control or silence opponents during the journalists' newsgathering efforts or as punishment for past coverage.

Media are, of course, social institutions, and both influence and are influenced by other institutions and the population. It has been observed that when terrorism strikes a society, the press either "apologizes for the current ruling groups or it becomes an advocate for oppositional groups whether elites or mass publics."[35] If the former course is pursued, state terrorism is ignored or excused. If the latter course is chosen, the media become targets for that terrorism. Even if a middle course is pursued, journalists can be forced into exile or otherwise discouraged from providing further information.

Foreign journalists are less likely than domestic journalists to be killed by state terrorism, but such deaths occur. Even when not directly targeted for attack, foreign reporters are regularly blocked in their efforts to get information from victims, government officials, or others knowledgeable about the terrorism.

Threats and actions against media personnel, combined with official silence about this type of terrorism, keep much news about such political violence from being widely disseminated. Peter Flemming and Michael Stohl have observed that "while sensational hijackings, hostage takings and cafe bombings have become a staple of most media reports on terrorism, the most heinous torture, mass disappearances, systematic killings and even genocide are generally all but overlooked."[36]

Even when state terrorism is covered, it is often treated as deviant and uncharacteristic action by government that is the result of unusual internal conflict or international disputes. Part of the problem in covering state terrorism is that officials of nearly all nations are willing to describe all political violence and warfare against themselves and nations aligned with them as terrorism but will not use that term and downplay reports of violence when they or their aligned nations are the perpetrators or locations of such violence. When journalists use officials for information about violence in allied nations or the violence perpetrated by their nation, they get little help or information in their reporting or their stories are significantly colored by the reported statements of the officials.

Edward Herman has noted this to be the case with U.S. press reporting of terrorism in nations in which the U.S. government has national interests. He argues that, because of difficulties in gaining official perspectives and the journalists' own complicity, media tread lightly on these acts of violence, even if their scale is large, but do not ignore them altogether. "The muted treatment of friendly terror gives the mass media more credibility as purveyors of 'all the news that's fit to print' than would total suppression," he says.[37]

Even when a democratic government gets involved in state terrorism, the government will make efforts to ensure that its involvement is not widely known or to inhibit future stories. In 1985, for example, the *Washington Post* revealed that Arabs trained by the CIA had tried to kill the radical Moslem leader Sheikh Muhammed Hussein Fadlallah in Beirut. The group had placed a car bomb in front of his headquarters. The explosive device killed eighty people passing by the scene but failed to kill the sheikh. Release of the story brought significant criticism of the *Post* from government officials, and other journalists, who argued that the coverage made the nation look bad and jeopardized national interests in the Middle East because disclosure could provoke retaliation.

UNAVAILABILITY OF INFORMATION. Many of the difficulties that media encounter in covering foreign state terrorism are endemic to their own patterns of newsgathering and coverage. Although media at times appear omnipresent, the major newsgathering organizations maintain few bureaus worldwide and rely upon few correspondents to write international news. Instead, they usually rely heavily on reports coming from domestic media and from other foreign news services for news leads that will result in the dispatching of correspondents to locations where news is occurring. In the case of state terrorism, domestic media are usually intimidated and either do not carry the reports or downplay their significance. The timidity of many domestic news organizations and journalists is understandable given the violence that is often directed against them in unstable or authoritarian nations.

International newsgathering is also constrained in its ability to cover state terrorism because of the lack of access to areas of conflict and the inability to locate credible news sources. Governments that engage in systematic violence often block entry of foreign journalists or restrict their travel. In addition, the official sources that journalists rely upon as credible news sources "know nothing" about the violence when asked and, thus, no information is forthcoming. Journalists also face a variety of problems when covering state terrorism including language and cultural difficulties, the distances required to travel to locations of events, the difficulties of transmitting reports back to their employers and audiences, and the manipulation of the communication by other interested parties.

If journalists talk with the embassy personnel stationed in countries where state terrorism is occurring, they can receive briefings on a situation, but this information is usually colored by the policies of the government the embassy represents and might contain misinformation and disinformation that supports the host country. Thus it is difficult to gain credible, authoritative information on such violence from any official source.

ATTACKS DURING NEWSGATHERING. Journalists are regularly targeted for attack when they cover incidents or issues in ways that anger interested individuals and groups. Attacks occur to halt newsgathering, particularly photography, during incidents that individuals do not wish covered, or in an effort to halt ongoing coverage. When civilians protested actions of the government of Haiti that were interfering with the election process in the summer of 1987, for example, government troops and Tontons Macoutes, terrorists linked to the regime of Jean-Claude Duvalier, began indiscriminate attacks on civilians in which scores of persons died. On July 3, at a rally during which military units attacked civilians, foreign journalists taking photographs were deliberately fired upon.[38] Reporters and camera crews scrambled for cover and managed to avoid being hit, but some suffered minor injuries and equipment was damaged in the attack.

Such attacks on journalists continued as the promised election approached. On election day, November 29, a television cameraman for a station in the Dominican Republic was killed, and journalists from the United States, Mexico, El Salvador, and Great Britain were wounded in deliberate attacks by armed gangs and soldiers. A New York–based independent human rights group, the Committee to Protect Journalists, reported that "journalists did not merely get caught in crossfire: the gunmen targeted them repeatedly, terrorizing both the local press and hundreds of foreign journalists who had flocked to Haiti to cover the vote."[39]

ATTACKS FOR PAST COVERAGE. Previous news coverage can also result in the targeting of journalists for attack. This occurs when subjects of news reports dislike the coverage carried in news media and then single out critical journalists as enemies and targets for attack. An example of this type of targeting of journalists occurred in Colombia in August 1987 when the names of nine well-known journalists were found on a list apparently constructed by death squads linked to that nation's military forces. One of those named has since been slain and six others have fled the South American nation. Journalists on the list had been actively covering the nation's so-called Dirty War against the Patriotic Union, a communist political party that has seen about five hundred of its leaders and members killed since 1986, and had linked death squads to the nation's military forces.[40]

In September 1986, Jose Carrasco Tapia, an editor of the Chilean weekly news magazine *Analisis,* was dragged from his home by armed men who wore civilian clothes and was later found dead, having been shot a dozen times. Tapia was a severe critic of the military dictatorship in the country and had once gone into exile after being detained by government forces. Opponents of Gen. Augusto Pinochet blamed the attack on government security forces noting that Tapia was taken from the scene in a van similar to those used by state security agents, that the country was under a curfew at the time of the attack, and that no one but police and military authorities were allowed on the streets at the time the attack took place.[41]

Summary

Governments, thus, have a variety of interests in the coverage given terrorism. Some of that interest is altruistic, reflecting the desire to protect citizens. Some of their concern is self-interest, based on desire to preserve their positions in society, to protect security forces combatting terrorism, and to portray their enemies as bad and their allies and themselves as good. All of these efforts influence and constrain coverage of terrorism and affect the meaning of news of terrorism.

6

Content and Meaning
of Media Coverage

ALTHOUGH MANY OBSERVERS have criticized media performance in covering acts of terrorism, few studies have been undertaken to explore what media actually say and do in their coverage. Most of the criticism is anecdotal, and little of it is based on systematic review of media content. Over the past two decades, fewer than three dozen studies have addressed the content of reports about terrorism in an organized fashion.

In analyzing the content of media reports on terrorism one needs to consider several general questions: (1) What exactly is being covered? (2) How is it being covered? (3) How extensive is coverage? and (4) How does technology get used to change the coverage? These questions are crucial to understanding the role of media in terrorism, and it is imperative that they be answered before significant criticism takes place. The research that exists does provide some answers to these basic issues and helps provide a better understanding of what information is being conveyed and how it is being reported.

Content of communication in and of itself is not the only concern of those who consider the messages conveyed. Equally important is the meaning of those messages, that is, the interpretations of the facts in the messages. The meaning of news of terrorism is crucial because it helps develop the perceptions of audiences about the world around them and the ways in which audiences relate to the actors in terrorism.

What Is Being Covered

Although the number of studies carefully reviewing media coverage have been limited, some findings about the types of terrorism getting coverage are becoming clear. First, state terrorism is generally ignored. Second, the amount of nonstate terrorism covered is limited. Third, news coverage concentrates on incidents and government issues, to the detriment of background information. And fourth, there is a similarity in what gets coverage among media.

STATE TERRORISM IS IGNORED. Although state terrorism is the greatest contributor to worldwide violence, the topic is rarely addressed by media in day-to-day coverage of political violence. As discussed in the last chapter, the difficulties of gathering information about such violence and standard industry practices of newsgathering interfere with the acquisition of information about state terrorism and thus remove it from the public agenda. Even when state terrorism is covered, the information is far more general than that for nonstate terrorism because it is generally linked to the release of reports on violence by human rights groups or to policy-based criticism of unfriendly nations by government officials.

Studies about media coverage of state terrorism are noticeably lacking in the literature, but this is not surprising because even general literature about state terrorism is sparse. Nevertheless, it is clear that media have ignored or significantly downplayed extensive state terrorism.

Michael Stohl has noted that even when large-scale state terrorism involving genocide, starvation, and mass murder occurs, it does not get extensive U.S. coverage because of lack of interest by media and government and lack of access. When more than 100,000 persons were killed in the Indonesian invasion and occupation of East Timor from 1975 to 1977, for example, only four *New York Times* stories dealt with the violence. When 250,000 Hutu tribesmen were killed by the Burundi government in 1972, only twenty inches of the *New York Times* was devoted to the violence, a particularly genocidal campaign in which the ruling tribe attempted to kill all adolescent and adult males. A similar lack of interest accompanied the killing of 50,000 civilians by the government of Equatorial Guinea from 1977 to 1979. In that instance, the *New York Times* devoted only seven inches to the violence.[1]

The lack of coverage of state terrorism in the media has been well recognized by scholars and other observers, but their criticism of that absence has not resulted in increased coverage. As a result of the dearth of coverage, the public gains a distorted picture of terrorism and its perpetrators, according to Alex P. Schmid and Janny de Graff: "The average news consumer gets the impression of a unilateral upsurge in mainly left-wing insurgent terrorism. Yet state terrorism is a much more serious problem. In terms of victims the state terrorism in Guatemala, for instance, has cost many more lives in one year than all the international insurgent terrorist incidents of the last ten years together."[2]

The lack of coverage caused by governmental constraints results in difficulties in addressing the issue of domestic state terrorism even after it is terminated. Frederick Schiff, in an important study of coverage of Argentinean state terrorism after the fall of military rule in 1983, notes that the press in that country has since provided coverage to substitute for the lack of coverage during the so-called Dirty War. Nevertheless, he notes a reticence on the part of the press to condemn social-institutional structures that provided military and security officials the power to undertake the terrorism that resulted in the death and disappearance of as many as eleven thousand persons. As a result of that desire to support institutions, "the preferred press impression is that perpetrators were state-sponsored individuals, not representatives of the military and police as institutions, even though they included senior commanders." He concludes, "Violations of human rights occurred as . . . routine pervasive activities ordered by legal authorities yet such acts were [explicitly treated as] excesses and implicitly [as] exceptions."[3]

COVERAGE OF NONSTATE TERRORISM IS LIMITED. The general lack of coverage of state terrorism does not come as a shock if one considers the general lack of coverage of nonstate terrorism, which does not involve the same difficulties of identifying violence as terrorism. As little as 2 or 3 percent of the incidents of nonstate terrorism that occur annually worldwide receive coverage in the U.S. press.

If one considers those terrorist events that received significant international media coverage since 1975, one begins to get a better idea of how little is widely reported (Table 6.1). Of the thousands of incidents that occurred during this period only about two a year received significant coverage and only about one every two years received extensive coverage in the United States. It is, of course, the impressions created by these major events and the massive coverage given to a few events that helps create mental images of terrorism.

Michael J. Kelly and Thomas H. Mitchell found that a very large number of incidents go unreported, even in the papers of record, because of strong regional biases that allow papers to ignore much of the terrorism that occurs outside of the region in which the papers are lo-

Table 6.1. Large-scale events receiving significant international coverage, 1975–1991

Year	Event
1975	Kidnapping of Peter Lorenz by Baader-Meinhoff group Seige of OPEC meeting in Vienna
1976	TWA hijacking to Europe by Croatian nationalists[a] Air France hijacking to Entebbe, Uganda, by PFLP[a]
1977	Hanafi Muslem seige at B'nai B'rith offices in Washington, D.C.[a] South Moluccans seize train in Netherlands Lufthansa Flight 181 hijacked to Mogadishu, Somalia, by PFLP
1978	Aldo Morro kidnapping/killing by Red Brigades
1979	U.S. embassy in Tehran seized[a] Earl Mountbatten killed by IRA Grand Mosque in Mecca seized
1980	Bologna train station bombed
1981	Anwar Sadat assassinated[a] Brig. Gen. James Dozier kidnapped by Red Brigades
1982	Washington Monument seige[a]
1983	IRA bombing at Harrods in London
1984	IRA bombing/Thatcher assassination attempt at Conservative Party conference
1985	TWA Flight 847 hijacked to Beirut[a] Air India Flight 182 bombed over Atlantic Colombia Palace of Justice seized by M-19 Rome and Vienna airports attacked by Abu Nidal group[a] *Achille Lauro* seized[a] Egyptair Flight 648 hijacked to Malta[a]
1986	Air Lanka (Sri Lankan) Tri-Star bombed at Colombo TWA Flight 840 bombed over Mediterranean[a]
1987	KAL Flight 858 bombed over Malaysia IRA bombing of parade stand at Enniskillen
1988	Kuwait Airways Flight 422 hijacked to Iran-Cyprus-Algeria[a] Pan Am Flight 103 bombed over Scotland[a]
1989	UTA Flight 772 bombed over Niger Lebanese President Rene Moawad assassinated
1991	IRA mortar attack on No. 10 Downing Street[a] Rajvi Gandhi assassinated by Tamil separatists[a]

[a]Extensive U.S. coverage.

cated. Their study of coverage in the *New York Times* and *Times* of London noted that even though American diplomats and businesspeople were regularly targets of well-organized terrorist groups in South America, "these groups consistently failed to attract the attention of the Western press" in the 1970s.[4]

The lack of interest of media in news of terrorism is illustrated by the small amount of coverage in the United States devoted to the bombing of the French Union des Transport Aeriens (UTA) Flight 772 on September 19, 1989. Although 171 passengers and crew died in the crash, the event did not receive extensive coverage in the United States—

as had the similar attack on Pan Am Flight 103—because it lacked proximity and occurred in a remote part of Saharan Africa, was not targeting Americans, and did not involve a U.S. aircraft, all prime requirements for extensive U.S. coverage.

Diminished coverage of terrorism by media in countries outside the location of the attacks was also found by Zoe Che-wei Tan in a study of the coverage of the Irish Republican Army in American, British, and Irish papers. That study found a lack of interest in covering day-to-day IRA terrorism on the part of both the *New York Times* and the *Times* of London.[5]

The importance of local and regional interest in news about incidents of terrorism was also found by Ronald D. Crelinsten in a comparison of *Times* of London and *New York Times* coverage and magazine articles indexed in the *British Humanities Index* and U.S. *Readers' Guide to Periodical Literature.* His study revealed that extensive coverage of significant IRA campaigns in 1975 and 1977 in the British paper and magazines was not present in the U.S. press and that a surge of U.S. coverage of terrorism in the first half of the 1980s was not mirrored in the British press.[6]

When nonstate terrorism is covered, reported incidents tend to be the most public and sensational acts of terrorism and generally must have strong and very apparent ties to the United States and its allies. Ongoing incidents in which photographic representations are available from television and still cameras and in which deaths occur are likely to be given more coverage than the most frequent type of terrorist act—the single incident, small-scale bombing or shooting in which deaths are limited. As a result, the largest number of nonstate terrorist acts go unreported (and continue to occur despite that lack of media attention), and discussions of terrorism coverage tend to focus on reporting of unusual terrorist events.

In his study of the coverage of terrorism in the *New York Times* and *Times* of London, Crelinsten compiled statistics that reveal that between 1972 and 1985 the U.S. paper devoted an annual average of two-tenths of 1 percent of its columnar inches to terrorism and related topics, while the British paper devoted less than one-tenth of 1 percent to the terrorism and related topics. In fact, during the fourteen-year period, each devoted an average of less than two hundred articles per year to the issue.[7] Although this indicates that an article, however brief, on terrorist acts and groups was published about every other day, the amount is far below the number the events of terrorism that occur annually.

COVERAGE EMPHASIZES EVENTS AND GOVERNMENT REACTIONS BUT NOT CONTEXT. When incidents of political violence are reported, the majority of time and space is devoted to describing or showing the event itself. When other aspects of such events are covered, media focus most strongly on government responses and reactions to the events or individuals or groups involved.

A study of the coverage of two European and one domestic terrorist groups on U.S. television, for example, found that about one-third of the coverage focused on the violence of incidents themselves and that government responses or concerns were addressed in nearly 40 percent of all the stories. Victims of that violence were also found to be key elements of the news reports.[8] Similar results were found in a study of television coverage of the takeover of the U.S. embassy in Tehran. David Altheide found that this emphasis on victims brought an overwhelming interest in the hostages and that nearly half of all topics covered concerned U.S. government actions and statements.[9]

In a study of U.S. television coverage of the hijacking of TWA Flight 847, Tony Atwater found slightly different percentages of time devoted to government reactions and victims, which suggests that as time passes—as in the case of the Iranian siege—government reactions and efforts receive more coverage due to the lack of other developments to report. Atwater's study found that the status of the aircraft hostages accounted for 34 percent of all coverage and that U.S. government reaction was the focus of 17 percent of the coverage. His study found that the television newscasts focused on terrorist demands and acts for only 7.5 percent of the coverage.[10]

A study of nine major *prolonged* incidents of political violence between 1982 and 1986 found that incident and government-related reports were dominant in major U.S. media and that there was a declining interest in events over time unless American citizens were involved as victims. The study concluded that initial reports on terrorist acts concentrate on incident reports—the who, what, when, and where aspects of the stories. This initial stage, which lasts two days, is followed by a second reporting phase in which government-related reports become dominant as the media report the diplomatic, political, and military responses made by government. The study found that in prolonged events a third stage occurs in which government-related reports continue to dominate, but background stories become strong as media attempt to convey how and why the events occurred.[11] This would seem to support the proposition that government reactions and efforts tend to become the focus of coverage as time passes.

The emphasis on official reaction and investigation can create confused and contradictory coverage, especially when multiple governments and agencies are involved. This was certainly the case as officials of the United States, the United Kingdom, West Germany, Finland, Malta, and other nations investigated the bombing of Pan Am Flight 103. Because officials of each nation wished to protect their interests, and because officials of competing agencies in single nations wished to do likewise, the media carried extensive speculation, theories, and conclusions, often from unnamed sources. Officials blamed the attack on numerous groups, airlines, airport officials, and intelligence agencies. In nearly every case the blame for not preventing the attack was put on nations or agencies other than the nationality or affiliation of the official speaking with reporters, and when differing groups were said to be suspect in the bombing, the suspicions were based more on policy interests of the country of the official laying blame than on hard intelligence. The effect of the contradictory and biased information was to leave audiences confused and angry at everyone involved—the bomber, the governments, and the airline.

Although there are indications that when prolonged incidents are covered the media begin to deal with the background and contextual aspects of the story, this does not appear to be the case in the coverage of the greatest majority of incidents covered. Paletz et al. found that in television coverage of Western terrorist organizations, less than 6 percent of all stories discussed goals or underlying social conditions contributing to the conflicts involved.[12] Their study of *New York Times* newspaper coverage found that nearly three-quarters of all coverage ignored causes or objectives and did not even name the perpetrators.[13]

A similar study, conducted by Decker and Rainey, of the Black September attack on Israeli athletes at the Munich Olympics and the takeover of the Washington, D.C., B'nai B'rith headquarters showed that the *Times* and the *Washington Post* coverage did not explain in detail the causes of the perpetrators and that "sympathetic" education of the public did not take place.[14]

Atwater's study of the TWA hijacking found that causal factors, cultural issues, and other background topics amounted to only about 3 percent of all network evening news coverage. "Little attention was focused on less dramatic topics such as a history of Lebanon and conditions which may have given rise to the TWA hijacking," Atwater noted.[15]

This researcher, however, found that in the majority of prolonged events, background information became an important part of coverage after about a week's worth of reporting had occurred. In these extended coverage periods, that backgrounding might well reflect the interest in the causes that developed because of the terrorist act, or the lack of

other new information on the incident, or government efforts that sur-
round the incident.[16] Prolonged incidents, of course, are the exception
rather than the rule.

The lack of background stories might be the result of lack of initia-
tive on the part of journalists. Jerry Levin, the Cable News Network
correspondent who was kidnapped by Islamic fundamentalists in 1984 in
an effort to free seventeen Shi'ite Moslems held in Kuwait for the 1983
bombings of the French and U.S. embassies and Kuwaiti facilities, said
that he expected during his captivity that the seizure of Americans would
bring extensive coverage of Middle East issues and was surprised that it
did not.

> I figured, once word got out, that the kidnapped Americans whose
> disappearance was still mysterious were being held hostage and all for
> the same purpose, that enterprising stories, analyses, and discussions of
> the root causes of the Middle East violence that caused our kidnappings
> would naturally follow. . . . But that kind of backgrounding hardly
> happened, because the administration was successful in perpetuating
> the myth from the summer of 1984 on for nearly a year that the reason
> for our disappearance still was a mystery—when it clearly was not.
> Even after it was clear that we were all being held for the same reason—
> exchange for the prisoners in Kuwait—the government was not
> forthcoming publicly about the situation. Ambassador Robert Oakley,
> head of counterterrorism at the State Department, explained to the
> hostage families last July 30 that since the press did not push and has
> not pushed for information and answers—the government did not and
> has not felt any obligation to volunteer any.[17]

The general lack of contextual and interpretative reporting of background issues is often due to the space, time, and financial constraints
placed on news operations. A study of broadcast news decision makers
by L. John Martin and Yossi Draznin has revealed that media managers
view their responsibilities in covering terrorism the same as they do in
covering all types of news. As a result, the emphasis is placed on getting
the facts about the events taking place and then, later, if there is time and
interest, on interpreting and explaining the events.[18]

Attributions of the causes of terrorist events in network television
coverage in 1986 and 1987 were biased, according to a study by Milburn
et al. The researchers found that coverage focused on internal, that is,
personality explanations for the violence, rather than on external, situational explanations for the events. This bias toward explaining terrorism
as the work of individuals with psychological and other disorders resulted from explanations of the events given by media personalities,

government officials, and authorities. The researchers also noted that when the United States was not the target of the terrorism, external, situational explanations were given, but that internal, personality explanations were given when the United States was attacked.[19]

A study that considered how one specialized, nonpopular media outlet has dealt with the issues surrounding terrorism has found that a broader, more explanatory approach is possible. Linda K. Fuller, exploring the treatment of terrorism in the *Christian Science Monitor* over a ten-year period, found that "the *Monitor* tells its readers not to get caught up in the emotionality of the news, but to be informed about the events and to be prepared to take educated stands. It is that emphasis on action, on problem-solving, that sets this newspaper apart."[20] The placement of emphasis on such contextual issues in the paper might indicate that it is a function of nonpopular media to provide such coverage rather than that of the popular news sources.

SIMILARITY IN COVERAGE. Coverage of acts of terrorism by major and popular news organizations shows a significant amount of similarity, undoubtedly due to strong professional norms that define news and influence the types of coverage given to various incidents. Altheide, for instance, found no significant difference in the coverage given by various television networks of the U.S. embassy takeover in Iran. Despite the fact that the incident lasted more than a year, his study found a similarity in terms of the number of reports, minutes of coverage, topics covered, and topics emphasized.[21] Tony Atwater's study of the TWA hijacking found the same result for that incident.[22]

Altheide has argued that, despite the presence of competing media, U.S. media presented a strongly homogeneous view of events that is damaging because "homogeneous messages by major news channels make it difficult for viewers who rely on these sources of information to discern the multiple realities underlying many issues and events . . . and then assess them."[23]

How Acts and Perpetrators Are Covered

Studies that have considered the reporting techniques and words employed in coverage of political violence have found that media appear to make efforts to be neutral or balanced in their reporting of terrorism and that when bias enters coverage it tends to favor social order and the status quo. These studies also reveal that drama and conflict are heightened in the coverage, that background information and explanation are not given emphasis, and that there is a similarity in how terrorist violence is covered by different media.

Warren Decker and Daniel Rainey, for example, explored how major newspapers covered the Black September attack on Israeli athletes at the 1972 Munich Olympics and the Hanafi Muslim takeover of the B'nai B'rith headquarters in 1977 and found that coverage of the events was neutral or negative, but never biased toward those engaging in the violence.[24] Milan Meeske and Mohammed Javaheri conducted a similar exploration of the extent to which U.S. television networks were biased in their coverage of the seizure of the U.S. embassy in Tehran. They found that nearly 80 percent of the sentences used in news reports were factual and verifiable; only 20 percent could be considered inferences or judgments. The researchers concluded that "the three networks tended to be mostly neutral whenever they made inferences or judgments."[25] Of the sentences containing inferences and judgments, two-thirds favored neither the United States nor Iran, and one-quarter of the total inferences and judgments favored the United States, a far smaller amount than expected.

This author and Paul D. Adams, in a related type of study, explored the characterizations made of acts and perpetrators in elite U.S. newspaper coverage of 127 terrorist incidents from 1980 to 1985. That research considered whether characterizations were made in nominal or descriptive terms. Nominal terms were straightforward descriptions with as few inherent judgmental qualities as possible about the acts or perpetrators; descriptive characterizations contained judgments about the acts or perpetrators within their denotative or connotative meanings. The research revealed significant differences in the ways media and government officials characterized acts and perpetrators. Members of the media and witnesses tended to use nominal characterizations to refer to acts and perpetrators, and government officials tended to use words that are more judgmental, inflammatory, and sensationalistic.[26]

Decker and Rainey found that *Washington Post* and *New York Times* coverage of the Black September and Hanafi incidents did not overly sensationalize the events but rather concentrated on informing readers about the ongoing events.[27]

Presentation of television news of terroristic political violence tended to emphasize sensational aspects and the immediacy of developments. Atwater, for instance, found that coverage of the TWA hijacking was dramatic, reactive, and extensive, findings that mirrored those of the study of the Iranian embassy takeover.[28] Altheide found that "on the whole, volatility and instability of the Iranian government was more characteristic of network evening newscasts than the less dramatic, but very important, historical, cultural and religious contexts of the Khomeini government."[29] Another study of the embassy takeover found that television placed great emphasis on immediacy and on-the-spot reports, even when little was taking place at the site. James Larson found that one-third of all television reports contained direct visual reports from Tehran.[30]

Paletz et al. found that the three terrorist groups they studied were covered similarly by TV organizations. "The three networks' coverage of the three groups [IRA, Red Brigades, FALN] was extremely similar. They reported the same events and depicted them similarly. Violence and government responses were emphasized; terrorists' goals, objectives, perspectives were neglected."[31]

A study of television coverage of terrorism from 1968 to 1971 by Sandra Wurth-Hough found that packaging of news of terrorism by the three major networks distorts the reality of terrorism, apparently for dramatic effect, and "conveys an overall impression of the omnipresence of violence." The study also revealed that the amount and kinds of coverage of terrorism overemphasized injury and death, thus giving an impression of terrorism that is not matched by the reality of most terrorist attacks.[32]

Dramatic elements have also been shown to be used in newspaper headlines, presumably with much the same results. Paul D. Adams found that although newspaper stories tended to use neutral language to describe terroristic events and perpetrators, such attempts to moderate the tone of stories were overshadowed by the use of descriptive, that is, judgmental, words when fatalities were involved. In nonfatal situations, regardless of location, intended target, or identity of perpetrators, headlines used more conservative wording. In fatal situations, more sensationalistic words, helpful in attracting reader attention, came into use.[33]

Another study on the use of the words *terrorism* and *terrorist* in the press found that the press will generally use the words in headlines only if there is a prevalent disposition against the group involved. That research, by L. John Martin, also found that reporters will quote persons calling the acts *terrorism* and perpetrators *terrorists* if the reporters are neutral or opposed to the group involved but will not do so if there is support for the group or its cause.[34]

Despite the emphasis on dramatic elements in the reporting of the events, Paletz et al. found that media reports regularly made efforts to reassure audiences by softening the threat in their stories and emphasizing the control and stability of government.[35] Thus, any destabilization of society desired by the perpetrators was reduced.

How Extensive Coverage Is

Although the greatest percentage of terrorism is not covered by the U.S. press because it is state terrorism or is nonstate terrorism that does not directly affect the United States, the American press regularly becomes enamored with specific incidents and provides massive and often overwhelming coverage of those terrorist acts.

When terrorist incidents become major news events due to the nature and the choices of news executives, there are significant indications that these stories are allowed to consume media time and space out of proportion to their social or political significance. This was true as early as 1977, during the Hanafi Muslim seizure of the B'nai B'rith headquarters in Washington, D.C. A review of the network newscast coverage of that three-day event found that about 40 percent of the total news time was devoted to the incident, with ABC devoting 30 percent, CBS devoting 30 percent, and NBC devoting 53 percent of their time to the building takeover.[36] The coverage thus pushed much national and international news off the television news agenda, diminishing the import of those stories—when their national and international impact could be expected to affect more persons than the takeover story—and increasing the import of the takeover.

Extensive coverage was also found in the case of the takeover of the U.S. embassy in Tehran. Networks, finding time limited during regularly scheduled newscasts, developed special reports and other forums to allow them to increase that coverage. ABC, of course, began using a late-night news-and-talk format that developed into the popular show "Nightline," which remains on the air today.

A study of coverage of violence and crime in Midwest U.S. media in 1976 and 1977 found that reports on political terrorism accounted for 5 percent of all news in newspapers and 8 percent of television news.[37]

Widespread media interest also developed in several terrorist incidents during the 1980s. Atwater, for example, found that the TWA hijacking and hostage taking became "the dominant news event covered over the [two-week] period."[38] An average of fourteen minutes per newscast, more than half of all the time, was devoted to the topic.

In 1987, when Korean Airlines Flight 858 crashed near the Thai-Burma border, it was covered both in the United States and Korea as a "normal" air crash, although officials alleged—without offering evidence—that the crash was the work of North Korean agents. Three days after the crash, two suspects were arrested for placing a bomb on the plane. Although both attempted to commit suicide, one survived and later admitted her part in the episode. After the arrests took place, coverage changed dramatically, and the press gave significant coverage to the terrorism issue. In Korea the terrorism aspect dominated the South Korean news. Coverage was so extensive that it pushed other news, including the upcoming Korean presidential election, off the front pages of newspapers for three days.[39]

The Korean experience would seem to indicate that devoting significant attention to certain events is not merely an American trait. This idea receives additional support if one considers the coverage of terrorism found by Mario Morcellini in a study of Italian television coverage in 1980 and 1981. His study found that news about terrorism accounted for 2 percent of coverage of news topics during the period examined.[40]

Occurrences in Japan in 1972 also add credence to the argument that interest in terrorism is not confined to U.S. and Western media audiences. After police raided the headquarters of the Red Army in Karuizawa, Japan, several members escaped but were trapped with hostages in a nearby home for ten days. When authorities decided to end the incident by storming the facility on the tenth day, three television stations halted regular programming and covered the event live for more than ten hours.

Proximity to communication facilities and media personnel undoubtedly influences the type and amount of coverage. George Quester, for example, argues that the hijackers of the *Achille Lauro* did not achieve coverage as extensive as the hijackers of the TWA aircraft because the ship's location at sea made it impossible for media to reach and record the scene.[41]

The importance of proximity to media is well illustrated by the hijacking of a Kuwaiti airliner in April 1988 by Shi'ites seeking the release of fundamentalist Moslems held in Kuwaiti prisons for bombings in Kuwait in 1983. Although no U.S. citizens were known to be hostages and there was no direct U.S. involvement in other forms, American media interest in the event increased dramatically when the plane reached Cyprus. During the first days of the incident, the hijacking had received relatively routine coverage. During a prolonged stopover in Iran, reports on developments—using some footage from Iranian television—were used, but the story was not emphasized in either broadcast or print media in the U.S. After the plane reached Cyprus, the situation changed significantly. Live television reports and increasing attention by print news organizations developed rapidly, well before the hijackers killed two Kuwaiti military personnel on board. The hijacking became the lead story in most network and local news broadcasts and moved above the fold on the first page of most newspapers. This change in coverage occurred because of an accessible satellite uplink facility on Cyprus and the presence of bureaus and facilities of the major U.S. television networks and international wire services on the island, which is used as a base for coverage of Lebanon. After the aircraft left Cyprus for Algeria, the news coverage diminished dramatically in both intensity and emphasis, undoubtedly because the networks and wire services did not maintain bureaus and significant numbers of personnel in that country.

Real Time Coverage Issues

Broadcast technology makes it possible for television and radio networks and individual stations to provide real time, that is, "live" reporting and coverage of events at the scenes of terrorist actions. This technology provides the ability to give immediate coverage, and that immediacy heightens the drama of the events underway. Through such coverage, especially television coverage, the audience is psychologically drawn into the ongoing event and becomes a part of it through the ability to observe it from a perspective similar to actually being at the location.

In years past, broadcasters relied upon film to record events, a technology that was later replaced with videotape. Both, however, required that the film or tape be transported back to the broadcast facility for airing so that there was a time lag between filming or taping and the broadcast of the material. The technology for live coverage of events has existed for all of the history of broadcasting, but such coverage required significant advance planning and movement of bulky equipment so that it was not efficient for live coverage of unplanned news events such as terrorist acts. This changed with the development of microwave technology that allowed remote cameras to broadcast live and recorded images, within a limited area, from news crews in the field to their stations for rebroadcast to the wider audience. Live coverage of all kinds of news events was now possible for both networks and local stations. The same principles of operation were extended worldwide with the development of satellite newsgathering (SNG) technology.

The development of SNG technology, however, increased the potential for terrorists to gather intelligence on what authorities do during events, because terrorists can watch or have observers watch the live coverage. Even if those who regularly cover hostage takings, hijackings, and related incidents are careful to protect sensitive information and the operations of authorities, the danger is heightened because this equipment is being put into the hands of younger, less-experienced journalists and technicians as it diffuses throughout the television industry.

The effect of this diffusion of technology on newsgathering techniques during terrorist events is not lost upon the industry, which is well aware of the increased ability it now has to cover terrorism. One trade publication has noted that

> for the first time, it [SNG technology] gives local stations the technology needed to report live or send videotaped stories from nearly anywhere. Unlike the fixed teleports in Cyprus and Damascus used by the networks to uplink taped reports of flight 847, SNG technology is completely mobile. Instead of taking your videotape to a teleport, you take the teleport to the story.
>
> Lightweight electronics and antennas designed for easy breakdown and packing into air cargo containers can be taken anywhere commercial airlines fly, packed in a vehicle, and taken to the site of a story.[42]

Microwave technology allowed local stations to provide live and taped coverage of events in their localities for many years, and, as indicated earlier, this technology resulted in release of sensitive information, interference with authorities, and live broadcasts of hostage situations that created significant concern among police personnel and media critics. The addition of SNG technology to media electronic tool kits now allows local stations to cover much wider areas, including the international arena, and many stations have begun using the technology when there are local ties to international events. In fact, a number of local stations have already used on-the-spot reporting in such situations, and this can be expected to increase as the use of SNG technology expands in the industry.

The use of satellite and microwave newsgathering technology by television networks and local stations also reduces the need for government officials and experts to explain and interpret events to the public because the audience sees the events for themselves. As a result, government officials' power to interpret and assign meaning to events might be diminishing, but the vision provided audiences is still limited by the location of cameras, the view of events they provide, and the extent of that coverage.

The Meaning of Coverage

Individuals experience the world about them through their senses, acquiring knowledge by processing information received by sight, hearing, touch, smell, and taste. When persons encounter the events of life, they do so with all the senses, and they construct a view of reality based on meaning conveyed through those senses. A witness of an act of terrorism sees the actions, hears the cries of panic and pain, feels the hardness of the floor as he or she seeks protection, smells cordite and blood, and tastes the perspiration of fear that rolls from his or her face.

When events of the world are not experienced firsthand, however, the sensory experience is limited. Individuals who are told about events even by direct observers acquire their knowledge of reality and ascribe meaning to the events based on limited information and sensory input. The interpretations these individuals place on events are significantly affected by the interpretations placed on the events by reporters and officials from whom they learned about the events. Secondhand observers do not see, hear, touch, smell, and taste an event in the same manner as those who have observed firsthand. Instead, they have a synthetic experience in which the meaning of the event and the data available are subject to the constraints and distortions inherent in the storytelling techniques and formatting used to convey the event, and to the selection of information. A person who is told about a violent act hears about it but does not see, smell, touch, or taste it. Individuals who see terrorism in visual images on television can see and hear only that part of the experience that is focused upon by the cameras and sound devices. He or she does not smell, touch, or taste the event. His or her information is thus limited, and the meaning the individual receives comes most strongly from those senses that are employed and from the significance assigned the event in the words of observers and officials.

Coverage of terrorist violence, as an act of communication, conveys not merely data about occurrences but meaning of the occurrences as well. Facts in themselves have no significance until they are shaped and framed in contexts that provide meaning and affect audiences' understanding. As a result, there is no single reality, but multiple realities that are constantly changing. Yet, individuals and nations seek to come to some consistent interpretations and definitions of reality in order to cope with the constancy of change and the inability to fully grasp what is real. Paul Watzlawick has argued that communication is the means by which reality is created and that individuals embrace accepted definitions of reality as a means of control:

> Our everyday, traditional ideas of reality are delusions which we spend substantial parts of our daily lives shoring up, even at a considerable risk of trying to force facts to fit our definition of reality instead of vice versa. And the most dangerous delusion of all is that there is one reality. What there are, in fact, are so many different versions of reality; some of which are contradictory, but all of which are the results of communication and not reflections of eternal, objective truths.[43]

The problem of understanding reality is particularly salient when dealing with sociopolitical issues such as terrorism because rarely do individuals within the same society interpret political issues similarly, and the problem is significantly compounded in international situations. The difficulties caused by differing perspectives that provide meaning to terrorist events have been pointed out by Thomas Cooper, who notes that "despite the feigning of objectivity and despite many journalistic crusades against ethnocentricism and racism, mainstream journalists largely partake of a world view in which terrorism is not associated with one's self but comes from 'the other.'" As a result, he argues, media audiences are able to look on others who use terror as inferior, less valuable, weak, or wrong.[44]

There is evidence that different media can help and harm the public's understanding of terrorism. Milburn et al. revealed that individuals who relied mostly on television for their news were able to make no explanation, or could give only simpler explanations, of the causes of terrorism than those who used other media.[45] Follow-up studies by Milburn et al., using survey and experimental techniques, also found that those relying upon television coverage had reduced understanding of terrorism and tended to attribute terrorism to problems in the personalities of perpetrators rather than to external factors.[46]

Patrick Clawson has noted that many journalists have particular difficulty in determining the differences between irregular warfare and terrorism:

> Judging what is or is not terrorism can be particularly difficult in the context of irregular war, such as those in Afghanistan, Central

America, or Southern Africa. Covering an irregular war requires sailing a true path between twin rocks. On one side, the siren Scylla entices reporters to describe as terrorism all actions in an irregular war, especially one that is unpopular. However, the terrible and usual anguish of war, including irregular war, differs considerably from terrorism.[47]

The difficulty of establishing what is irregular warfare and what is terrorism is, of course, compounded when the sirens of political government try to label all such violence *terrorism*.

Even if participants or observers did not try to directly influence the mediated meaning of terrorist events, the meaning of the events would be influenced by the techniques used to tell about the incidents. David Altheide has observed that

the mass media provide publics with important information about events and their meaning for our lives. Ironically, perhaps, we need to be aware of the role such media play in editing and distorting the information we receive when visual imagery on TV can give an impression that what is being seen is what is most significant, particularly when these reports involve "terrorism."[48]

Thus, distortion caused by media communication of acts of terrorism results from several factors including (1) the selective use of labels and the word *terrorism* to identify acts and perpetrators and (2) the rhetorical traditions and formats used by journalists in conveying information.

SELECTIVE USE OF LABELS. It is a trite but valid observation that, by both accident and design, "one man's terrorist is another man's freedom fighter." This occurs because the perspectives of observers who ascribe meaning to acts color their analyses of terrorism and their choice of words to describe the acts. The English language itself helps color any description of acts and perpetrators of violence because it is steeped in a culture that stresses permanence and nonviolent social change. As a result, attempts to bring about change through violent means are most often described in words that have highly charged connotations even if balance is desired by those telling about acts of terrorism. Reports about such efforts must often carry negative connotations merely because of the words selected by media and other observers.

This problem occurs in all coverage of conflict but is heightened in the coverage of elements of terrorism. In describing those who take part in or are affected by the violence, journalists seek to provide a sense of who is involved or affected. The presentation nearly always favors one side over another through words that reflect the orientation of American culture. When hostilities occur in other nations, the words most often used reflect the values of reporters and the ideology of the United States. This problem is manifested even in the description of state apparatuses. In Anglo-American connotation, the very word *government* is one of legitimacy, and the word denotes the governing individuals and apparatuses that are presumed to be legally and, thus, "morally" constituted. The word is normally used to encompass all the institutions officially linked to the state. Nevertheless, members of the media and officials regularly use other biased words to refer to governments they deem less desirable. The word *regime* is often used to convey less legitimacy, and the term *dictatorship* conveys the specter of authoritarianism and one-person or military rule. The use of these words is inconsistent, however. Although U.S. media regularly label the apparatuses of communist, socialist, or non-U.S. aligned nations *regimes* or *dictatorships*, such designations rarely appear in reports about pro-U.S. nations, despite the large number of authoritarian and military governments that maintain power with very little public support.

These difficulties of labeling the state pale by comparison to those found in reports on individuals engaged in antigovernment violence. The biggest difficulty arises because these individuals often do not wear uniforms or bear the validation and legitimization of the term *soldiers*. Instead, regardless of the nature of the state they are opposing, they are usually described by words that bear less desirable connotations because they involve violent opposition to the status quo: *rebels, insurgents, terrorists, guerrillas,* and *revolutionaries*.

The word *rebels* denotes those who oppose existing "legitimate" government but does not connote support for or against any particular ideology. It is not as negative a word for those who seek social change as is *revolutionaries,* which now connotes individuals with the purpose of ideologically motivated change in the structure of society. The word *guerrillas* is overused and denotes individuals who engage in violent activities that are predominantly aimed at government-owned or -operated facilities or the economic infrastructure of a nation and who use guerrilla tactics, that is, hit-and-run attacks. Guerrillas generally do not possess heavy weapons or maintain distinct battle lines or positions. The levels of authority and organization within guerrilla groups are usually not as clearly defined and visible as they are in more traditional military and paramilitary organizations. A problem in using the term *guerrillas* developed in the reporting of the Israeli invasion of Lebanon and the subsequent siege of Beirut in 1982. Throughout much of the fighting, correspondents referred to Palestine Liberation Organization combatants as guerrillas, despite the fact that they were an organized, uniformed fighting group with military bases and facilities and with specific battle positions and were engaged in relatively standard military operations during the hostilities. To term them *guerrillas* was inappropriate for the situation, although it might have been appropriate for some PLO operations within Israel.

The word *insurgent* does not seem to convey the strongly negative connotations that other terms do because it has been used much less, connotes less-organized or fewer ideological opponents to the existing military and civilian authorities, and seems to suggest a lower level of violence. It is used most often when referring to groups that oppose governments that are not on friendly terms with the United States. Afghan resistance groups and anti-Sandininta organizations have been regularly referred to by government officials and members of the press as *insurgents, rebels,* or *contras.* Similar groups that oppose governments aligned with or supported by the United States are more often characterized by stronger, more negative descriptions. The word *terrorist* is greatly overused and is often misused in referring to violence against government. Government officials use the term and deny all justification for violence against the government as a means of gaining support against rebels.

Reports about conflicts are thus often biased by the descriptions of the events and the participants to convey specific meanings to media audiences. This can be deliberately done through the manipulation and use of words by observers to whom the media turn for reaction and explanation. It can also stem from inherent media bias. Journalists' attitudes and values influence their characterizations even if they attempt to portray events with some balance. The cultural and ideological beliefs of journalists and the societies to which they belong affect how they experience and report on the world and thus affect the meaning of events conveyed to their audiences.

Edward C. Epstein has noted that members of American media organizations use the word *terrorism* to label opponents as a means of supporting government policies and achieving a political consensus that permits policies to be put into action that might otherwise be rejected. Epstein writes, "One of the most common means of creating approval for particular aspects of that policy is the use of political labeling. By using emotionally positive terms to describe supposed friends of the United States and emotionally negative terms to malign enemies, journalists cue the American public on what their papers portray as desirable attitudes."[49]

As a result, says Epstein, antigovernment violence against U.S.-supported states is depicted as terrorism, but similar violence against states not supported by the United States is not. This occurs because the media present the views of government policy makers and other interested parties who support the official views.

A study of the use of the word *terrorist* in the Turkish press between 1976 and 1980 also found the selective use of the term. During that period the term was used by the mass circulation center and right-wing newspapers to refer to left-wing political violence. Similarly, the left-wing press used the term to refer to right-wing political violence.[50]

Thomas Cooper has shown that, when discussing world events, both Soviet and American media personnel use the *terrorist* label in similar fashions to describe some actions of each other's governments and allies. This type of "adversarial perspectivism" thus allows them to report on the same event with one side labeling it an atrocity and terrorism and the other side labeling it justifiable conflict.[51]

Lyn Fine and David Rubin, however, argue that the use of the word *terrorism* might not be a strictly "us" and "them" phenomenon but, instead, might be linked to ideas of legitimacy in superpower confrontations. The use of *terrorism* and *terrorist* is limited in U.S. media in references to the acts of the Soviet Union and its Warsaw Pact allies and might likewise be restrained in referring to U.S. and NATO actions, they contend, because "terrorism as a frame now seems reserved only for individuals, sub-national groups, and pariah states (or states that one of the superpowers would make into a pariah)."[52]

Crelinsten has found that use of the words *terrorism* and *terrorist* by media to frame acts of political violence began about 1972 and was well established by the early 1980s in both the United States and Britain. Previously, media indexing and description of such violence was made using descriptions of tactics — such as bombings, shootings, kidnappings — or the locations in which they took place. He argues that the adoption of this frame for political violence followed the lead set by the increased interest in political violence and representation of such violence as terrorism by security officials in the late 1960s and early 1970s.[53]

Picard and Adams's study of characterizations made of acts and perpetrators of terrorism revealed that government officials worldwide extensively use words that are judgmental and inflammatory to ascribe meaning to acts of violence. Words such as *brutal, criminal, despicable, murder,* and *terrorism* are regularly used to ascribe meaning to such acts. The perpetrators are *brutal, cowards, criminals, evil, extremists,* and *terrorists.*[54]

It should also be noted that when the violence is directed against those to whom government officials object, similar acts resulting in injury and death are often described as *unfortunate* and *unintentional* and perpetrators are described neutrally as *armed men or women, attackers, commandos,* or more supportively as *freedom fighters* or *patriots*. Terms that describe the actors as being in opposition to something disagreeable to prevailing orthodoxy, such as *anticommunist group* or *antifascist,* might also be used.

Although major popular and elite media operate similarly and appear to provide similar meaning to groups and acts of terrorism, other types of media operate with different social perspectives that provide alternative labeling of acts and perpetrators. Judith Buddenbaum has shown this to be the case in coverage of the Namibian Independence Movement and the South West African People's Organization. In a study that compared *New York Times* coverage to that of the Lutheran World Information press service, she found that "the images created by the two bodies of coverage are strikingly different." This occurs, she argues, because the two news organizations rarely cover the same events and issues and have very different sources of information. The *Times* relied upon government and official sources for news and interpretation, while the religious news service relied upon missionaries, church workers, and other persons living and working in the region.[55]

RHETORICAL TRADITIONS AND FORMATS. Journalists have traditionally employed four rhetorical traditions in conveying news, and these also affect the meaning received by audiences. First is the information tradition, which emphasizes factual information and documentation of events. When this is employed, a calm, dispassionate conveyance of information occurs. Such "raw journalism" is often found in initial news reports of terrorist events. The second tradition, sensationalism, is emotional. Material is presented in ways that emphasize alarm, threat, provocation, anger, and fear. This type of presentation, which is used in a variety of types of reporting, works well in the reporting of conflict and terrorism because the subject is likely to bring an emotional response and contains inherently dramatic and tragic elements that can be sensationally reported. The third journalistic tradition of storytelling is that of the feature story, which contains significant symbolism and often focuses on individuals as heroes or villains, victims or perpetrators. This type of story focuses on individuals to provide a context that helps to put news events and larger issues into a personal perspective. In the reporting of terrorism, this can take the form of stories about what it was like to be a hostage or what it is like to live in a repressive nation in which individuals are striking out at the government. The fourth tradition, the didactic approach, stresses explanation and education about how and why things work. Articles about the tactics of terrorists or authorities often fall into this category.

Which of these traditions is utilized helps to determine the meaning conveyed about the events. A dispassionate approach will result in a less emotional response or lessened fear on the part of the reader. A sensationalist approach can increase fear and, not incidentally, improve newspaper sales and television viewership. An approach emphasizing violence and threat might make the news appear more significant than does an approach that downplays such violence. A news report about any incident can be constructed by employing any of the traditions (Figure 6.1), and which tradition is selected depends upon the reporter and editors involved.

Also important to understanding the coverage of terrorism is the role of formats, that is, presentation conventions that are used to package information and that determine the significance and the information that news packages carry. Elements of such formats are the focus of the report, the sources of information, and the actual means by which these and other elements are presented. The focus of the report determines the type of information about an occurrence that is presented. It can involve description of an event, factors influencing an event, analysis of an event, and so on. These types of focuses are found in both print and broadcast reports of terrorist incidents. The number and types of sources of information are also parts of news formats. In most situations reporters attempt to get information from representatives of all significant parties involved. In cases of terrorism, however, this generally means finding an official government spokesperson and, perhaps, a victim if one can be reached.

Print and broadcast formats diverge when it comes to the means by which information is packaged for delivery to audiences because of the inherent differences in the media of delivery. Spatial and temporal elements of the two media differ significantly; these influence how information is provided and thus influence the structure and amount of information delivered. Newspapers, for example, devote *space* to information, while broadcasting media devote *time* to information. Graphic devices for presenting and illustrating information are used in both media, as are photographic representations. Television, however, utilizes video and live representations that are unavailable to print media, and thus TV can convey information with more immediacy and urgency.

On television, several types of packaging formats are typically used

INFORMATION TRADITION

Four persons were killed and thirty-three others injured when a bomb exploded in a cafe in downtown Paris Thursday.

SENSATIONALIST TRADITION

A terrorist bomb ripped a crowded Paris cafe Thursday, mortally wounding four persons and leaving thirty-three persons covered with blood from their injuries.

FEATURE STORY TRADITION

A couple on their honeymoon was killed Thursday when a bomb destroyed a Paris cafe. The bride and groom, who had been married for less than twenty-four hours, were among four persons killed and thirty-three wounded when the bomb exploded.

DIDACTIC TRADITION

The bombing of a Paris cafe Thursday is believed to signal a new wave of violence by Moslem fundamentalists angered by French foreign policy in the Middle East.

6.1. Sample leads for news stories using different rhetorical traditions.

to deal with terrorist incidents: news bulletins, newsbreaks, newscasts, news magazines, current affairs talk shows, and documentaries. Each has its own conventions for use of materials. News bulletins, for example, are generally unanticipated short breaks in programming during which the news reader provides brief details of a currently occurring event. Newsbreaks are similar to news bulletins but are generally one- to two-minute news broadcasts that occur at regularly scheduled times; newscasts are the regularly scheduled news shows; news magazines include shows that devote significant time, often ten to twenty minutes, to a single story; current affairs talk shows are characterized by relatively lengthy interviews by journalists with officials and other newsmakers; and documentaries are explorations of significant topics that devote as much as two hours to developing and exploring different aspects and perspectives on those issues.

In considering the impact of media portrayals of terrorism, it is important to understand the differences in these formats, the types of messages they carry, and their potential impact on audiences. Understanding these differences is crucial because most critics of terrorism coverage consider information conveyed in news shows but ignore other types of news media formats. It has been noted that "there is a readiness to assume that news coverage is the paradigm case of all actuality television. The main consequence of this assumption is to limit your understanding of how the television system as a whole works."[56]

Format differences exist in newspaper coverage. Presentation formats include news briefs; shorts; first-day stories, second-day and follow-up stories, news features; and interviews. News briefs are typically one-paragraph–long summary stories that are often placed in sections for international, national, or regional news. Shorts provide slightly more information in two to five paragraphs and are found in the regular news columns. First-day stories are the typical event-oriented news stories that most people identify when thinking of current news in newspapers. Second-day and follow-up stories are used to update events and occurrences since the first report. News features approach events and issues by placing them in a context through the use of human interest approaches, profiles of individuals and groups, background information, and analysis of developments and their meaning. Occasionally newspapers and news magazines publish interviews in a question-and-answer format if editors deem the persons interviewed and the specific answers to be so important that they warrant this format rather than a regularly constructed story.

The dominant portrayals of terrorism on television come in the forms of news bulletins, newsbreaks, and newscasts; and most newspaper reports are briefs, shorts, and first-day reports. In both media, audiences receive short, staccato presentations that provide little contextual information and emphasize dramatic elements of conflict, threat, and casualties. Fred W. Friendly has observed that "hyping the slightest details as 'news breaks' and 'Extra editions' distort[s] the news rather than put[s] it in context. Lack of context and texture are the deadly sins that deform the best intentions of fairness."[57]

The emphasis on short news reports makes it possible for the public and governments to significantly misunderstand events. James Larson has argued that news coverage of Iran before the fall of the shah, which consisted mainly of short news items, did not deal with political opposition in any systematic way; when violence was covered, reporters did so in ways that denigrated the opposition's importance and support.[58] As a result, audiences received a mistaken view of the strength of the opposition, and the collapse of the government surprised many.

The developments that surrounded the formation of the new Iranian government and the seizure of the U.S. embassy were also reported in a way that distorted the meaning of the events, according to Robin Wright, who says that reporters were

> so preoccupied with the Iranian hostage situation that [they] didn't report the revolution. It would have been useful if, instead, the media had focused on the dynamics and the developments within the revolution rather than just standing outside the U.S. Embassy. And that's one of the reasons the Americans by and large didn't understand the importance, the magnitude of that revolution and how it could change history. By 1985, the media had grown up and begun to understand that the Shi'ite phenomenon was a major one in the region and had to be understood in order to cope with it realistically.[59]

The themes and issues consistently addressed in coverage of terrorism also cast meanings upon news that have effects upon the perceptions of audiences. In their coverage of the seizure of the U.S. embassy, for example, reporters focused extensively on the policies and actions of the U.S. government. Patricia R. Palmerton has argued that the coverage conveyed the meaning that U.S. government actions helped cause the seizure to take place. Coverage of the Carter administration's prolonged and ineffectual actions to end the takeover also conveyed an image of powerlessness that the Iranians were pleased to exploit.[60]

Despite those critical views, there is evidence that media did not depart significantly from official views and policy in dealing with the incident. David Altheide has argued that both the content and style of television coverage supported administration policy during the event and

that reporters, acting as intermediaries, were used as diplomatic channels for communication with the Iranian government and militants holding the embassy personnel hostage.[61]

In another study, Palmerton argued that two overriding themes
found in CBS Evening News coverage of the Iranian situation reinforced
terrorist strategy by focusing blame on officials and promoting a repressive response. She contends that the network's overriding thematic
focuses were institutional causes of the incident and the suggestion that
military intervention would reestablish control.[62]

A study of the rhetoric of President Carter regarding the situation
found that an overwhelming ethnocentric emphasis to the detriment of
explanatory information might have made it difficult for the public to
understand his administration's policies in handling the situation and
kept the public from understanding the significance of the event and its
causes.[63]

The image of the president and the leaders of Iran created by media
rhetoric were examined by Ralph Dowling, who found that the Iranians
were portrayed as opportunistic or irrational and that President Carter's
image was split. Some members of the media portrayed him as strong,
good, and restrained, while others portrayed him as weak, selfish, and
ineffective.[64]

Jack Lule has studied media portrayals of victims of terrorism by
focusing on the mythical elements found in news reports. A study of the
coverage of the killing of Robert Dean Stethem during the hijacking of
TWA Flight 847 and of Leon Klinghoffer during the hijacking of the
Achille Lauro found that reporters provided rhetorical visions that
portrayed the victims as symbolic sacrifices in a manner that provoked
intense identification with the victims by audiences.[65]

The application of rhetorical studies to news coverage of terrorism
is in its infancy, and application has been limited mainly to a few major
incidents of terrorism. These few studies, however, suggest that significant messages about terrorism are exceptionally important in understanding the effects of mediated portrayals of such events. The rhetorical
visions created about the Iranian incident undoubtedly contributed to
the image of President Carter that resulted in his failure to win reelec-
tion. They also helped to arouse anti-Iranian sentiment during the period, and coverage of the airline and cruise ship incidents since that time
has undoubtedly helped to increase the view of the madness of terrorists
and heightened the threat felt by individual Americans. This is, of
course, where significant implications to public policy become clear. The
meaning created by rhetorical aspects can promote fear and demands for

reprisal and prevention. Given that most coverage does not provide background information and context, uneducated public opinion can thus sometimes push governments into actions that are undesirable in the long run or that contradict knowledge held by officials.

Summary

Acts of terrorism are covered both better and worse than many observers have asserted. Those who employ political violence get far less coverage than many believe. Only a small percentage of nonstate terrorism gets covered, and state terrorism is generally ignored. Thus, we must conclude that the "commit violent act, get coverage" theory is less factual than its proponents believe. The lack of coverage of state terrorism, however, radically distorts the image of terrorism. This omission makes nonstate terrorism appear to be a far greater threat than it actually is and keeps the public from realizing that about ninety-five out of one hundred terrorist victims are casualties of state terrorism.

When terrorism is covered, there is not much variation in what is reported and how it is reported by journalists for major American media because they operate similarly and follow standard professional norms. The predominant coverage emphasizes action, violence, and government views, and provides little information that increases public understanding. In cases of prolonged incidents, some background and contextual material appears, but this is often colored by official views of the situation.

Although coverage is provided for a relatively small percentage of terrorist events, specific events capture the fancy of media managers and coverage of those events becomes overwhelming. Because a lot of coverage is provided of a few terrorist events, perceptions of terrorism and media handling of terrorism are often linked to those events. Thus, the handling of those events conveys great meaning to audiences about terrorism.

Studies of media coverage of terrorism have shown semantic differences in the way acts and perpetrators of terrorism are handled, but there appears to be an overall effort by news organizations to be relatively neutral. Government officials, however, make efforts to direct references to acts and perpetrators in a negative direction when they oppose the groups committing the acts and to direct references in a positive direction when they support the acts and perpetrators.

Important contributions to the presentation and meaning of information conveyed in media result from the formats in which the news is presented. Whether these presentations tend to be sensational and dramatic or dispassionate and educational depends to a great extent on these formats. Unfortunately, the formats most often employed and to which most audiences are exposed are those that provide the least information and tend to provide a somewhat distorted form of information.

7

Implications of
Media Coverage

ACTS OF TERRORISM concern authorities and the public because they create both first- and second-order effects. First-order effects are the carnage and casualties caused by the violence. These effects present immediate needs for official responses to care for victims and to resolve continuing incidents. Second-order effects are the broader social effects of terrorism.

First-order effects are the main element of terrorism that concerns most members of the public and the police, security, and medical authorities. Although some security measures can be taken and repressive policies implemented to reduce the possibility of attacks and first-order effects, no society can completely insulate itself from terrorist violence.

Second-order effects are of less concern to the public, but of significant concern to policy makers and terrorist strategists because of their potential for legitimizing and promoting causes and groups that engage in political/social violence. It is out of concern for second-order effects that the role of media in terrorism becomes the focus of criticism and study by officials and social observers. The ability of media to rapidly convey the messages of terrorists, generate public reactions, and place meaning on the acts leads some policy makers—unable to prevent many attacks—to look at means of constraining or restraining media coverage as means of reducing second-order effects.

Terrorism is, of course, a dramatic symbolic means of demonstrating power. Mass media have a unique ability to amplify and widely disseminate that message. This capacity for carrying messages of the effectual exercise of power raises the greatest concerns in discussions of the role of news coverage of terrorism. Power, of course, is manifested in a variety of ways, including direct physical control and influence on the attitudes and opinions of individuals.[1]

In the case of terrorism, power is clearly demonstrated by direct physical power over individual victims. The violence, whether it be bombings, shootings, or hostage takings, symbolizes this type of control, especially when persons are killed in the process. It is through this exercise of control that terrorists hope to have some influence on the public by generating awareness and recognition of the group and its goals. If the acts do not persuade the public of the worthiness of the cause and its supporters, some terrorists hope that the violence will make the public fearful of the group so the terrorists must be taken as a serious participant in and threat to the social milieu. This, of course, raises doubts about the ability of the existing social order to survive without change.

The main factors promoting terrorist actions are group dynamics developed in the formation of dissident organizations, the perceived illegitimacy of regimes opposed by groups and the public, and the availability of training and weapons support. Once groups develop and gain such support, internal and external communication techniques can be employed to promote group status, provide internal psychological gratifications to group members, and provide avenues of communication to target audiences—functions that can be carried out using media channels.

Many critics of terrorist communications activities, however, have unrealistic views of the power of media as communication channels and ignore how communication takes place even without media. As this book has demonstrated, the simplistic argument that terrorism takes place because of media coverage is clearly without foundation. It is only necessary that *communication* take place to serve terrorist strategy, and such communication is not dependent upon media. The difficulty of maintaining the argument that media are to blame becomes clear when one considers the terrorism that occurs in authoritarian and totalitarian societies where governments exercise strong control over media. The argument is also problematic because television requires that the audience have the technology to receive broadcasts and print media require the audience to be literate enough to read the content. In much of the world where widespread terrorism occurs, even in nations without authoritarian control of media, neither technology nor literacy are widespread among the populations. This lack of media does not stop awareness of the violence from spreading, however, because people discuss the attacks with their neighbors, friends, and relatives, and the violence becomes a topic for storytellers and minstrel singers and theater groups.

Even when media are widely available, they have far less effect than many critics have assumed. Part of the problem with the argument of media omnipotence is the media's limited effectiveness as a tool of persuasion. Another problem is the fact that many critics view the functions, uses, and credibility of different media similarly. These assumptions provide mistaken views of media usefulness to terrorists because the different news media do not operate similarly or serve the same functions for their audiences. Although television, radio, newspapers, and magazines convey information, they serve distinctly different needs and are used in very different ways by audiences. Differences in frequency and the ability to immediately convey information result in media being used in different ways during news events. In addition, the general functions of media help determine how information, even news, is conveyed. Newspapers and magazines, for example, serve primarily information and idea functions, whereas broadcast media serve primarily entertainment functions. The differences in immediacy and approach to information help characterize and differentiate the manner in which news is conveyed in the media. Overall, television and radio do not provide the range or amounts of information provided by newspapers and magazines, and they tend to present information in a more popular and entertaining form than do newspapers and magazines.

When terrorist incidents are covered by media, the types of coverage given are characterized by these inherent differences in media operations and the functions they serve for audiences. But the coverage does provide audiences with a view of the world that helps audience members develop knowledge about terrorism and terrorist groups. That knowledge about acts and perpetrators is significantly distorted, however, because of media decisions and coverage patterns and manipulation of that coverage by terrorists and governments.

A major contributor to this distortion is the process of selecting information that will become "news" in media reports. Most reports of terrorism that reach media never get broadcast or printed. National media, particularly television networks and newspapers of record, tend to carry more information about terrorism worldwide than do regional or local media. But even national media appear to cover no more than 2 to 3 percent of incidents of nonstate terrorism and provide even less information about state terrorism. If one considers the broader picture of political/social terrorism, probably less than 1 percent of all incidents gain coverage in the national media, and far less is reported in the regional and local newspapers and broadcast news programs that most of the public use for news about the world.

Distortion of the scope and nature of terrorism also occurs because media coverage is reactive rather than anticipatory. Media personnel tend to wait for things to happen and then begin reporting on what happened, and if the occurrence is significant enough or garners a great audience, reporters explore how and why the event occurred. Efforts to promote contextual understanding of events are absent for the most part, and determination of the meaning of the events is usually left to social authorities. It is rare that reporters for major media organizations take the time to explore issues and ideas that might be leading to problems.

An *event-oriented* rather than *idea-oriented* concept of journalism is predominant in Western media, especially major media in the United States. As a result of the media ideology that defines news mainly as events, ideas and issues are not often conveyed and discussed unless they are first linked to occurrences that can be recorded as event news. As a result of dependence on events as the determination of what gets covered, individuals and groups seeking media access have learned to create what Daniel J. Boorstin has called "pseudo-events," that is, contrived events designed to solicit media coverage in order to gain attention.[2]

The event-centeredness of media reporting also has the effect of keeping reporters from exploring trends in social disorders in various parts of the world. As a result, audiences, including authorities, are forced to confront terrorism at the micro rather than the macro level. This makes it possible for authorities to argue that society must deal with the manifestations of social problems—that is, the acts of terrorism and their effects—rather than the social problems themselves.

The types of reports in which news about terrorism is conveyed in newspapers, magazines, radio, and television, and the ability of governments to restrain or halt certain types of information as an effort to promote social control over terrorism, also alter the view of terrorism that audiences receive. This is especially true in terms of broadcasting because electronic media throughout the world, even in the most liberal of democracies, is legally controlled by government. This type of control is generally imperceptible to audiences, and they only occasionally become aware of the distortion that occurs when disputes about control are made public. It has been noted that "the representation of 'terrorism' on television is constrained not only by the different kinds of programme form available but also by the complex modes of control and pressure which the state and the wider political establishment can bring to bear on broadcasting."[3]

Legal approaches to media coverage of terrorism fall into three patterns: an authoritarian pattern, which directly forbids coverage; a democratic pattern, which protects free expression and provides only marginal control; and a criminal pattern, which makes certain types of coverage illegal. Patty Millett has observed that

> the severity and comprehensiveness of a nation's legislation in this area depends on a number of factors, including the type of government (democracy, authoritarian); the extent of the terrorist threat (sporadic; quasi-war); the nature of the terrorist threat (sectorial, those that seek total destruction of the state); and the traditional relationship between the press and the state (independent-adversarial; state-controlled–cooperative). Balancing these considerations has resulted in a wide range of legal controls on the media's coverage of terrorism. At one end of the spectrum, the press suffocates in a legal morass of censorship and access restrictions. In these instances, the legislation often has a dual character: it stifles coverage of insurgent terrorism and, simultaneously, mobilizes the press as an instrument of state terrorism. At the opposite end of the spectrum, almost absolute freedom exists for the press, with only limited exceptions for national security. In between these two extremes operates a wide variety of regulatory schemes. Some have expressly targeted the press in their general anti-terrorism legislation, while others simply employ specific provisions of their general criminal law against wayward members of the media.[4]

In addition to efforts to restrain coverage they dislike, government authorities regularly make great efforts to characterize the symbolic terrorist acts in ways that support their policies and the existing social order. Media normally give extensive coverage to these views and interpretations. George Gerbner has noted the effectiveness of government control in assigning meaning to these symbolic acts:

> Symbolic uses benefit those who control them. They are usually states and media establishments, not small-scale or isolated actors or insurgents. Though perpetrators of small scale acts of violence and terror may occasionally force media attention and, in that sense, seem to advance their cause, in the last analysis such a challenge serves to enhance media credibility ("just reporting the facts") and is used to mobilize support for repression often in the form of wholesale state violence and terror or military action, presented as justified by the provocation.[5]

Despite such problems of distortion, some media coverage provides important information about the world. The hijackers of TWA Flight 847 brought to the attention of the world the fact that Israel was holding thousands of Lebanese in detention camps and that even the U.S. government was opposed to the Israeli action. The jailing of these individuals was certainly important before the hijacking, but media did not attach significance to and address the problem until the hijacking made the issue salient as news. Similarly, efforts by Tamil separatists to gain a homeland that respects their religious beliefs received little coverage in the West until members of a Tamil group bombed a Sri Lankan airliner, thus elevating the conflict to the news agenda.

Although there are relatively few occasions in which background material and context are provided in news coverage and distortion of events is limited, media can nevertheless provide information that helps the public gain some knowledge of the world and the events that take place around them. Gabriel Weimann argues that coverage that conveys information and generates knowledge is important:

> In the case of terrorism, the media's decision to cover or not may be crucial for the public's knowledge about the event and its background. How many of us would know about the Croatian call for independence, about the Palestinian problem, about the South Moluccans, about the Armenian desire for recognition of the Armenian Holocaust—if all were not reported, analyzed, and explained by the media, following terrorists events? Moreover, it is not only the coverage that informs us but sometimes its absence that creates ignorance and denial.[6]

News coverage of terrorism also provides important information about the events to government officials. During the first twenty-four to thirty-six hours of most significant terrorist events, authorities rely upon news coverage for basic information about what is happening, and most admit that the information is generally accurate and useful. Once government officials have reached the location of an incident and organized their efforts, the news media become less important to them but remain important for the public.

Patrick Clawson has argued that the media's contributions to government and public information are one reason that more, rather than less, coverage is needed. Reducing coverage, he maintains, would hurt authorities' abilities to combat terrorism:

> In times of a hostage-taking crisis, media coverage can provide public officials with vital information, since the media often have greater ability than U.S. officials to get close to the action and to report in quickly.

During a hostage crisis, Cable News Network (CNN) can provide more up-to-date information than the State Department or CIA. Reporters also have greater access to the terrorists themselves, who often refuse to speak to government officials. For precisely these reasons, the government already relies on CNN and other electronic media for fast-breaking news. By using this information rather than duplicating it, the government can devote more resources to analyzing information and putting it into context.[7]

Because of the importance of media-generated information, officials in the White House, the Departments of Defense and State, intelligence services, and other agencies regularly monitor the major television networks and wire services for breaking news and information, even when terrorist incidents are not underway.

Many critics of terrorism coverage argue that the news functions that make the government and the public aware of terrorist acts and groups and their causes provide a reward for violence. But most available evidence indicates that knowledge cannot be equated with support for the groups or their actions. In fact, most of the indicators reveal that the more the public knows about terrorist groups, the less likely they are to support the groups. Despite media attention, public opinion surveys consistently show that the public is opposed to terrorism and rejects the acts as a means of achieving ends.

This result is not surprising because news coverage tends to support accepted social norms, and studies indicate that coverage does not support groups committing violence. A study of U.S. television coverage, for example, refuted the idea that the coverage enhanced the legitimacy of those groups or other groups covered by media. The authors found that

> terrorists enjoy attention, but they are not endowed with legitimacy by television news. . . . The justness of the terrorists' causes are denied. Most of the stories about the insurgents' actions are provided by the authorities and concern governmental responses to the violence, or the actual terroristic acts themselves. The underlying objectives of the violence are rarely explained, almost never justified. Terrorists' tactics are stressed in television news. When tactics are emphasized without discussion of motives, objectives, goals, or precipitating social conditions, then context is discarded, and political justifications are denied. The terrorists are identified with criminal violence and seen simply as bent on terror.[8]

News coverage of terrorism, however distorted by its omissions and promotion of the status quo, does provide some information that helps interested members of the public to comprehend what is occurring. That interest, of course, is dependent upon what is salient to the population. Public interest in reports of terrorism, as in any news, is influenced by the degree to which the news is perceived to affect the public. This, of course, is also a central factor in the determination of what topics and events get media coverage. Audiences whose lives are touched by the terrorism, or whose interests are attacked or supported by the violence, generally have greater interest in and knowledge about the precipitating conflict. Another factor contributing to knowledge is use of media. Individuals who spend more time acquiring information through media are, not surprisingly, likely to have greater knowledge of factors related to incidents.[9]

Reporting of terrorism can clearly serve the goal of promoting public fear and disorientation. News and entertainment programming can create an inordinate fear of violence in audiences after prolonged and repeated exposure to media portrayals of such violence. Persons continually exposed to crime and other violence on news and entertainment shows over a long period tend to fear victimization and to experience greater anxiety about the risks of violence than do those persons exposed to fewer media portrayals of violence. Thus, such portrayals of violence can engender alienation, mistrust, and fear.[10] Although little research has specifically focused on the audience effects of terrorism coverage, it is reasonable to conclude that results similar to those for news of crime and other violence would occur. Thus, repeated exposure to terrorism reports would be expected to lead to increased fear and mistrust among some members of the audiences.

There is evidence, however, that the generation of fear by the reporting of violence can be reduced if coverage places specific acts of violence into perspective by helping audiences understand the origins of the acts and the potential risks to the public at large. According to Anthony Doob and Glenn Macdonald, when the public understands the background of specific violent acts, anxiety levels are reduced.[11] The fact that media generally provide little contextual information about the causes of terrorism is especially disturbing in light of such findings. Because the media normally report on terrorism in short, incident-oriented reports, and only occasionally look behind the headlines, media audiences get a diet of information that undoubtedly raises anxiety and serves some goals of terrorists.

In addition to spreading fear, some media coverage has clearly interfered with officials' efforts to cope with specific incidents of terrorism and has provided the attention and recognition desired by some who have committed acts of violence. These problems of media coverage of terrorism have led some authorities to call for restraints on the press that conflict with the principles of liberal democratic society and, in fact, provide terrorists with a type of repression that some seek in the furtherance of their goals. This reaction should not be unexpected, however, because when faced with threats there is often a temptation for members of a society to yield to impulse, to place blame hastily, and to respond forcefully. Many government officials are more than willing to place the blame for terrorism — and their inability to predict and prevent such violence — on the media, attempting to restrict media operations as a means of absolving their powerlessness to end attacks.

The British government, for example, has the ability to control media coverage through the Prevention of Terrorism Act, intended to help control violence related to Northern Ireland. The act makes it possible to require journalists to notify authorities before they have contact with groups engaged in violence, to report any unplanned contacts, and to provide copies of materials to the authorities. Security officials can deny permission for material to be carried by media if they deem it harmful. This limitation of press activity, it is argued, is necessary to reduce tensions by halting publicity and propaganda that might lead to further violence.

In the 1970s, the Argentinean government, responding to domestic terrorism, launched a massive assault on dissidents as a means of restoring order. Before the campaign was over, government forces and paramilitary units supported by government had seized and killed nearly ten thousand people — political, labor, and human rights activists; students; faculty; and critics — in the "Dirty War" that ultimately led to the downfall of the government in 1983. After journalists reported or criticized the early actions of the state's campaign of repression, they became targets as well, and soon Argentinean media no longer reported and scrutinized government actions. Innocent civilians and the society itself suffered from the state's actions.

These two examples of repressive government responses, differing widely in degree, show how media can become the focus of government interest and can be used as scapegoats in efforts to control terrorism. Halting media coverage and allowing unfettered government action against terrorists is not the answer to terrorism. In fact, forbidding media coverage altogether could *increase* the scale and amount of violence by those intent on gaining recognition, demanding access, and forcing coverage. If coverage were halted, demands for coverage would undoubtedly become negotiating points in some hostage-taking situations;

and when the coverage was provided, it would be under terms stipulated by the terrorists, a situation worse than responsible, unfettered media coverage.

Yonah Alexander has argued against halting coverage because of the potential for promoting more violence. He notes that "any attempts to impose media blackouts are likely to force terrorists to escalate the levels of violence in order to attract more attention. . . . Since a major goal of terrorism is to undermine authority and cause anarchy, an unjustifiable limitation or even destruction of free media will ultimately result in the victory of terrorism."[12]

Reduced coverage could also lead to misunderstandings and promote fear greater than that created by coverage. This would be expected to occur because the lack of authoritative information would lead to the public accepting less credible and less knowledgeable sources of information that could convey misinformation, exaggeration, and rumor. Katharine Graham, chair of the board of the Washington Post Company, argues that "terrorist acts are impossible to ignore. They are simply too big a story to pass unobserved. If the media did not report them, rumors would abound. And rumors can do much to enflame a crisis."[13]

Authorities, particularly political figures, who argue that communication should be controlled when groups use terrorist techniques often do so out of a sense of frustration because they have been unable to halt terrorism, and it becomes and remains a political issue that can harm support for elected officials and administrations. Security personnel and terrorism scholars tend to make less sweeping demands for media control—except in cases where operations might be directly jeopardized—because they believe the problem of terrorism can never be fully solved but rather is a problem to which governments and societies must adjust and which they can only partly inhibit. J. Bowyer Bell reflects this view when he notes that acts of terrorism "are more easily tolerated than prevented."[14]

Even if societies could meet the majority of demands of terrorist groups in the world today, some individuals and groups demanding change would not be satisfied. The social problem would not disappear because it is impossible for societies to meet all demands of those with grievances, so some oppositional groups would continue to exist and continue to develop.

Officials' frustration over media coverage of terrorism is manifest even when specific violence is not underway. They argue against, and some attempt to halt, media coverage of groups and individuals who have used terrorism techniques, interviews with representatives of the groups, and other coverage of the causes of violence. Thus, some authorities attempt to deny forums whether oppositional groups are nonviolent or violent. This situation is illustrated by the U.S. government's orders in 1988 to close the Palestine Liberation Organization's offices at the United Nations and to shut the PLO information office in Washington, D.C., orders that were challenged and overturned in the federal courts.

The tactic of denying a voice to violent groups when they are not engaged in an act of terrorism is problematic. History has shown that terrorism campaigns often reverse their scale and decline after major public actions, the development of interest in the perpetrators, and access to media is provided. An important school of thought suggests that media coverage might well be used to reduce the possibility of future violent action by removing the need for groups to resort to violence in order to gain attention. Thus, denying access might increase violence.

The view that coverage might reduce terrorism is not held solely at the fringes of the terrorism research community. Nevertheless, it receives little support among political officials and many of those to whom they turn for advice in combatting terrorism. Abraham H. Miller notes the major elements of this communication-as-preventative view: "If terrorism is a means of reaching the public forum, violence can be diffused by providing accessibility to the media without the necessity of an entry fee of blood and agony."[15]

Another argument in favor of complete and serious coverage of terrorist violence was put forth by the (U.S.) Task Force on Terrorism and Disorders. The group said, "The media can be most influential in setting the tone for a proper response by the civil authorities to disorders, acts of terrorism, and political violence. It can provide an outlet for the expression of legitimate public concern on important issues so as to act as a safety valve, and it can bring pressure to bear in response to public sentiment in an effective manner to redress grievances and to change official policies."[16]

The task force also argued that "the news media should devote more, rather than less, space and attention to the phenomena of extraordinary violence."[17] The group concluded that if such coverage avoided glamorizing the perpetrators of violence, provided reliable information, and gave appropriate emphasis to the consequences of violence, coverage would increase public understanding, reduce fear, and assist in reducing violence.

The group reached these conclusions despite the fact that it generally accepted the discredited stimulus-response view of media effects.

While admitting that no authoritative evidence directly linked media and violence, members of the task force did believe that the media influences potential perpetrators of violence and that coverage of such violence affects the ability of authorities to respond.

If frustration and despair lead to rebellion, and if those who rebel are denied forums in the media because the media support the dominant social order, then one must conclude that normal media channels are regularly denied significant dissidents. Thus, the only possible avenues left for gaining a media forum in which to communicate are acts designed to force their way into the forum. Violence is an effective means of achieving this, a fact of which we are painfully aware.

Two psychologists who conduct research on terrorism, Jeffery Rubin of Tufts University and Nehemia Friedland of Tel Aviv University and the Project on Terrorism at the Jaffee Center for Strategic Studies, recently argued that governments should help provide access to the media, which in most nations are government operated or government related. According to Rubin and Friedland,

> government should . . . try to reduce the destructiveness of terrorism by making it clear that a less dramatic performance will suffice to get the desired audience attention. Cameo appearances, for example, might be invited or encouraged as a substitute for full-scale productions. Imagine if Yasir Arafat or George Habash were to be invited to meet the press on Israeli television to express their views on what they consider to be political reality in the Middle East. Such an arrangement would provide these actors with the element of legitimacy they seek and would air issues without resorting to anything more violent than the savagery of the Israeli news media.[18]

As with most of the theories about the role of media in terrorism, there is little supporting evidence bolstering the theory of free expression as a means of controlling violence. The theory has merit, however. In recent years, the IRA, the Basque ETA, the Red Army Fraction, Al Fatah, and other groups have been granted platforms to express their views in interviews and other exchanges. A study of the behavior of these groups after their interviews could help determine whether terrorists regularly become less violent after being provided a forum. Such appears to have been the case with Yasser Arafat's supporters after international forums began to be provided to the PLO in the 1970s.

Many groups engaging in violence in order to convey messages to government, to the public, and to their supporters would undoubtedly find that the prospect of such access to media meets their needs. As Ralph Dowling has noted, using violence to gain media access reduces the possibilities of carrying out significant discourse on the issues but provides the ability to use the rhetoric of fear to achieve recognition in a different manner.[19]

As a means of reducing violence, opening the media to alienated, disenfranchised groups seems preferable to nearly every other option, but the chances of the idea being widely accepted are very slim. Managers of media organizations would be reluctant to risk offending audiences, losing revenue, and being accused of supporting terrorists. A measure of the potential for such condemnation can be seen in the criticism heaped on NBC by other media and journalists after the Abul Abbas interview in 1986.

In addition, the media are not likely to convey much information that conflicts with the views of their governments because they generally reflect their governments' perspectives when they deal with the issue of terrorism. The media are not an opposing force to authorities when terrorism occurs. The media support the existing social, political, and economic order in which they operate because they are part of and benefit from that order, and the views they convey rarely stray far from the norm.

This is not to deny there are problems, and there are clearly steps that can be taken to help reduce the problems experienced and caused by media reporting of incidents of political violence. Education about the nature of terrorism, about the problems and issues facing officials, and about the political and social antecedent to and the milieux of terrorism can help promote self-restraint and more complete reporting. Consideration of the effects of the limited amount and types of terrorism that are reported will help journalists understand the view and distortions of the problem they are giving audiences. Openness and candor between officials and media about potential problem areas during incidents have been useful and should be encouraged.

Lowndes Stephens has argued that media need to be more careful and critical of their selection and presentation of information about terrorism to ensure that media do not interfere with government operations but still represent the interest of the public by providing a less distorted view of the phenomena. He notes, however, that

responsible balanced coverage of terrorists' events is not simply a matter of cooperating with government authorities and avoiding becoming a player in negotiations or a pawn of the terrorists. The Reagan administration's arms-for-hostages deal with Iran—a country on our Department of State's list of countries sponsoring terrorism—and recent revelations regarding the FBI's illegal investigation of the Committee in

Solidarity with the People of El Salvador, a group opposed to administration policies in Central America—tell us the press must play a role as watchdog/fourth branch of government.[20]

The answer to difficulties posed by media coverage is not to kill, gag, or "kneecap" the messenger, but to help make the messenger more sensitive to the way it delivers information and to the content and impact of its messages.

Notes

CHAPTER 1

1. L. John Martin, "Violence, Terrorism, Nonviolence: Vehicles of Social Control," in *Social Control for the 1980s: A Handbook for Order in a Democratic Society,* ed. Joseph S. Roucek (Westport, Conn.: Greenwood Press, 1978), 186.

2. Alex P. Schmid and Janny de Graff, *Violence as Communication: Insurgent Terrorism and the Western News Media* (Beverly Hills, Calif.: Sage Publications, 1982), 15.

3. These arguments are commonly found in both popular and specialized publications on the subject of media and terrorism. See, for example, Michael J. O'Neill, *Terrorist Spectaculars: Should Television Coverage Be Curbed?* (New York: Priority Press, 1986); Robert A. Friedlander, *Terrorism and the Media: A Contemporary Assessment* (Gaithersburg, Md.: International Association of Chiefs of Police, 1981); and Abraham Miller, *Terrorism, the Media and the Law* (Dobbs Ferry, N.Y.: Transnational, 1982).

4. Yonah Alexander, "Terrorism, the Media and the Police," *Journal of International Affairs* 32(1978):101.

5. See Fred S. Siebert et al., *Four Theories of the Press* (Urbana: University of Illinois Press, 1956); William Hachten, *The World News Prism: Changing Media, Clashing Ideologies* (Ames: Iowa State University Press, 1981); and Robert G. Picard, *The Press and the Decline of Democracy* (Westport, Conn.: Greenwood Press, 1985), especially 57–71.

6. See Frederick J. Hacker, "Contagion and the Attraction of Terror and Terrorism," in *Behavioral and Quantitative Perspectives on Terrorism,* ed. Yonah Alexander and John M. Gleason (New York: Pergamon Press, 1981), 73–85; and Alex P. Schmid and Janny de Graaf, *Violence as Communication: Insurgent Terrorism and the Western News Media* (Beverly Hills, Calif.: Sage Publications, 1982), especially 117–37.

7. See Martha Crenshaw, "The Causes of Terrorism," *Comparative Politics* 13(July 1981):379–99; Amy Sands Redlick, "The Transnational Flow of Information as a Cause of Terrorism," in *Terrorism: Theory and Practice,* ed. Yonah Alexander et al. (Boulder, Colo.: Westview Press, 1979), 73–95; and American Legal Foundation, *Terrorism and the Media* (Washington, D.C.: American Legal Foundation, 1985).

CHAPTER 2

1. For a discussion of the semantic difficulties of words used to describe those who engage in political violence, see Robert G. Picard, "Words on War and Conflict: Political Bias Creeps into Reporting on Foreign Conflicts, Often Unintentionally," *St. Louis Journalism Review* (September 1983):21–22.

2. Richard Clutterbuck, *The Media and Political Violence,* 2d ed. (London: Macmillan, 1983).

3. See *Patterns of Global Terrorism,* published annually by the U.S. Department of State in the 1980s. The figures for different types of government employees involved in terrorism have been combined in order to yield the total percentage of government employees victimized by acts of terrorism and the relative proportions of groups such as diplomats, military personnel, and other officials.

4. This number excludes military personnel killed in combat zones, such as the Marines killed in Lebanon, which are more properly categorized as deaths due to acts of war than to terrorism.

5. Martha Crenshaw, "The Causes of Terrorism," *Comparative Politics* (July 1981): 396.

6. Ibid.

7. Ted Robert Gurr, *Why Men Rebel* (Princeton, N.J.: Princeton University Press, 1971).

8. Leon P. Baradat, *Political Ideologies: Their Origins and Impact* (Englewood Cliffs, N.J.: Prentice-Hall, 1979), 5.

9. C. A. J. Coady, "The Morality of Terrorism," *Philosophy* 60 (1985).

CHAPTER 3

1. For a discussion of the main elements of structural functionalism, see Robert Merton, *Social Theory and Social Structure* (Glencoe, Ill.: Free Press, 1949).

2. See Brian Barry, *Sociologists, Economics and Democracy* (London: Collier-Macmillan, 1970).

3. J. Herbert Altschull, *Agents of Power: The Role of the News Media in Human Affairs* (New York: Longman, 1984).

4. Neil C. Livingstone, *The War against Terrorism* (Lexington, Mass.: Lexington Books, 1982), 59.

5. For a compilation of his sociological and historical views, see Ibn Khaldun, *The Mugaddimah: An Introduction to History,* trans. Franz Rosenthal, ed. N. J. Dawood (Princeton, N.J.: Princeton University Press, 1967).

6. See Herbert Spencer, *Principles of Sociology,* ed. Stanislav Andreski (London: Macmillan, 1969).

7. For discussions of this approach, see Ludwig von Bertalanffy, "General System Theory," *General Systems* 1(1956):1–10; "General System Theory: A Critical Review," *General Systems* 1(1962): 1–20; and James G. Miller, "Living Systems: Basic Concepts," *Behavioral Science* 10(1965):193–237.

8. David Berlo, *The Process of Communication* (New York: Holt, Rinehart, and Winston, 1960), 24.

9. For an excellent discussion of the use of clandestine radio, see Lawrence C. Soley and John S. Nichols, *Clandestine Radio Broadcasting: A Study of Revolutionary and*

Counterrevolutionary Electronic Communication (New York: Praeger, 1987).

10. For important discussions of this stimulus-response approach, see Harold D. Lasswell, *Propaganda Technique in the World War* (New York: Alfred A. Knopf, 1927); and Elihu Katz and Paul Lazarsfeld, *Personal Influence* (Glencoe, Ill.: Free Press, 1954).

11. See Elihu Katz, "Communications Research and the Image of Society: Convergence of Two Research Traditions," *American Journal of Sociology* 65 (1960): 435–40.

12. An excellent discussion of the two-step flow theory is found in Elihu Katz, "The Two-Step Flow of Communication: An Up-to-Date Report on an Hypothesis," *Public Opinion Quarterly* 21(Spring 1957):61–78.

13. For a discussion of the balance model see F. Heider, "Attitudes and Cognitive Organization," *Journal of Psychology* 21(1946):107–12; for a discussion of the congruity model see Charles E. Osgood and Percy H. Tannenbaum, "The Principle of Congruity in the Prediction of Attitude Change," *Psychological Review* 62(1955):42–55; for explication of dissonance theory see Leon A. Festinger, *A Theory of Cognitive Dissonance* (Evanston, Ill.: Row, Peterson, 1957) and *Conflict Decision and Dissonance* (Stanford, Calif.: Stanford University Press, 1964); and for discussions of coorientation theory see Theodore M. Newcomb, "An Approach to the Study of Communicative Acts," *Psychological Review* 60(1953):393–404; and Keith R. Stamm and W. Barnett Pearce, "Communication Behavior and Coorientational Relations," *Journal of Communication* 23(September 1971):208–20.

14. See Jack McLeod et al., "Another Look at the Agenda-Setting Function of the Press," *Communication Research* 1(April 1974):131–66.

CHAPTER 4

1. Martha Crenshaw, "The Causes of Terrorism," *Comparative Politics* 13(July 1981):379.

2. L. John Martin, "Violence, Terrorism, Nonviolence: Vehicles of Social Control," in *Social Control for the 1980s: A Handbook for Order in a Democratic Society,* ed. Joseph S. Roncek (Westport, Conn.: Greenwood Press, 1978), 186.

3. Hugh Rank, *The Pep Talk: How to Analyze Political Language* (Park Forest, Ill.: Counter-Propaganda 1984), especially Chap. 4.

4. See Hadley Cantril, *Gauging Public Opinion* (Princeton, N.J.: Princeton University Press, 1947), especially 220–30.

5. An excellent compilation of this and other tested principles of persuasive communication are found in Marvin Karlins and Herbert Abelson, *Persuasion: How Opinions and Attitudes Are Changed,* 2d ed. (New York: Springer Publishing Co., 1970).

6. S. E. Rada, "Trans-National Terrorism as Public Relations?" *Public Relations Review* (Fall 1985): 32.

7. Paul Kecskemeti, "Propaganda," in *Handbook of Communication,* ed. Ithiel de Sola Pool and Wilbur Schramm (Chicago: Rand McNally College Publishing, 1973), 844.

8. David Drescher, "A Typology of International Political Communication: Factual Statements, Propaganda and Noise," *Political Communication and Persuasion* 4(1987): 88.

9. Jacques Ellul, *Propaganda: The Formation of Men's Attitudes* (New York: Alfred Knopf, 1965).

10. For discussions of needs and their importance in motivating human beings, see Abraham Maslow, *Motivation and Personality* (New York: Harper and Row, 1970).

11. "Terrorism Is Likely to Increase," *London Times*, 25 April 1975.

12. Ronald P. Lovell, *Inside Public Relations* (Boston: Allyn and Bacon, 1982), 346.

13. George H. Quester, "Cruise-Ship Terrorism and the Media," *Political Communication and Persuasion* 4(1986):360.

14. "Death at Dinnertime," *Time,* 22 April 1985, 36.

15. Peter J. Boyer, "Arab's Interview Stirs News Debate," *New York Times,* 7 May 1986, A7.

16. Related at the Poynter Institute for Media Studies Seminar, "Hostage Taking and the Media: The Challenge of Coverage," St. Petersburg, Florida, 22–24 January 1987.

17. Peter W. Kaplan, "Competition over Hostages Is Fierce for the U.S. TV Networks in Beirut," *New York Times,* 20 June 1985, A17.

18. Frederic B. Hill, "Media Diplomacy: Crisis Management with an Eye on the TV Screen," *Washington Journalism Review* 3(May 1981):23–27.

19. Robert G. Picard, "How Violence Is Justified: Sinn Fein's *An Phoblacht,*" *Journal of Communication* 41(Fall 1991):90-103.

20. Quoted in Neil Hickey, "Terrorism and Television," *TV Guide,* 31 July 1976, 4.

21. See Richard Clutterbuck, *The Media and Political Violence,* 2d ed. (London: Macmillan, 1983).

CHAPTER 5

1. Stuart Hall et al., *Policing the Crisis: Mugging, the State, and Law and Order* (London: Macmillan, 1978), especially 57.

2. Ronald Crelinsten, "Power and Meaning: Terrorism as a Struggle over Access to the Communication Structure," in *Contemporary Research on Terrorism,* ed. Paul Wilkinson (Aberdeen, Scotland: Aberdeen University Press, 1987).

3. See "Guidelines of United States Government Spokesmen During Terrorist Incidents" in Abraham Miller, *Terrorism, The Media and The Law* (Dobbs Ferry, N.Y.: Transnational, 1982), 148–50.

4. Capt. Brent Baker, "The PAO and Terrorism," *Military Media Rev.* (July 1986): 10.

5. James LeMoyne, "Human Rights Aide Slain in Salvador," *New York Times,* 11 December 1987, A12.

6. Paul Delaney, "PLO Chiefs Meet to Mourn a Comrade and Plot Strategy," *New York Times,* 18 April 1988, A8.

7. "U.S. Backs Kuwait and Cyprus," *New York Times,* 12 April 1988, A13.

8. Rodeina Kenaan, "Bomb Kills 54, Injures 125 in Lebanon," *Boston Globe,* 24 April 1988, 1.

9. Quoted in Deni Elliott, "Family Ties: A Case Study of Coverage of Families and Friends during the Hijacking of TWA Flight 847," *Political Communication and Persuasion* 5(1988): 67–75, 71.

10. M. Cherif Bassiouni, "Problems in Media Coverage of Nonstate-Sponsored Terror-Violence Incidents," in *Perspectives on Terrorism,* ed. Lawrence Z. Freedman and Yonah Alexander (Wilmington, Del.: Scholarly Resources, 1983), 195.

11. See J. Chester Stearn, "News Media Relations during a Major Incident," *Police Journal* 4(October 1976):257–60.

12. See *New York Times,* 11 November 1979, 1.

13. Paul Lazarsfeld and Robert Merton, "Mass Communication, Popular Taste and Organized Social Action," in *The Process and Effects of Mass Communication,* Rev. ed., Wilbur Schramm and Donald Roberts (Urbana: Univ. of Illinois Press, 1974), 554–78.

14. Gabriel Weimann, "The Theater of Terror: Effects of Press Coverage," *Journal of Communication* 33(1983):44.

15. Ibid., 43.

16. Josephine Holz et al., "The *Achille Lauro:* A Study in Terror" (Paper presented to the American Association for Public Opinion Research, Hershey, Pennsylvania, 14–17 May 1987).

17. David L. Paletz et al., "The IRA, the Red Brigades and the F.A.L.N. in the *New York Times,*" *Journal of Communication* 32(Spring 1982):162–72; and David L. Paletz et al., "Terrorism on TV News: The IRA, the FALN, and the Red Brigades," in *Television Coverage of International Affairs,* ed. William C. Adams (Norwood, N.J.: Ablex Publishing, 1982), 143–65.

18. Robert G. Picard and Paul D. Adams, "Characterizations of Acts and Perpetrators of Political Violence in Three Elite U.S. Daily Newspapers," *Political Communication and Persuasion* 4(1987):1–9.

19. Joel Bellman, "BBC: Clearing the Air," *The Journalist* (January 1986):20.

20. Peter J. Boyer, "Arab's Interview Stirs News Debate," *New York Times,* 7 May 1986, A7.

21. "Thatcher Urges the Press to Help 'Starve' Terrorists," *New York Times,* 16 July 1985, A3.

22. The problems with the existing research and suggestions of social science techniques for undertaking research to answer the questions raised about media as the contagion are found in Robert G. Picard, "News Coverage as the Contagion of Terrorism: Dangerous Charges Backed by Dubious Science," *Political Communication and Persuasion* 3(1986):385–400.

23. Rudolf Levy, "Terrorism and the Mass Media," *Military Intelligence* (October–December 1985):35.

24. *Terrorism and the Media* (Washington, D.C.: Washington Legal Foundation, n.d.), 24.

25. Larry Grossman, "The Face of Terrorism," *The Quill,* June 1986, 38.

26. Manus I. Midlarsky et al., "Why Violence Spreads: The Contagion of International Terrorism," *International Studies Quarterly* (June 1980):276.

27. Edward Heyman and Edward Mickolus, "Observations on 'Why Violence Spreads,'" *International Studies Quarterly* (June 1980):299–305.

28. Quoted in Alex P. Schmid and Janny de Graaf, *Violence as Communication: Insurgent Terrorism and the Western News Media* (Beverly Hills, Calif.: Sage Publications, 1982), 143.

29. Brian M. Jenkins, "The Psychological Implications of Media-Covered Terrorism," *Rand Paper Series* P-66276, June 1981.

30. Franco Salomone, "Terrorism and the Mass Media," in M. Cherif Bassiouni, *International Terrorism and Political Crimes* (Springfield, Ill.: Charles C. Thomas, 1975), 43.

31. Richard Clutterbuck, *The Media and Political Violence,* 2d ed. (London: Macmillan, 1983), 191.

32. M. Cherif Bassiouni, "Problems in Media Coverage of Nonstate-Sponsored Terror-Violence Incidents," 178.

33. "Death Toll for Journalists Rises to 34 in '87," *Presstime* (January 1988):41; see correction in letters, *Presstime* (February 1988):75.

34. Committee to Protect Journalists, *Attacks on the Press 1987* (New York: Committee to Protect Journalists, 1988).

35. Frederick Schiff, "Rewriting State Sponsored Terrorism: The 'Dirty War' Reinterpreted by the Press in Argentina during the Period of Democratic Transition" (Paper presented to the Communication in Terrorist Events Conference, Boston, Massachusetts, 3–5 March 1988).

36. Peter A. Flemming and Michael Stohl, "State Terrorism and the News Media" (Paper presented to the Communication in Terrorist Events Conference, Boston, 3–5 March 1988).

37. Edward S. Herman, *The Real Terror Network: Terrorism in Fact and Propaganda* (Boston: South End Press, 1982), 51.

38. Joseph B. Treaster, "Calls Grow, amid Violence, for Ouster of Haiti's Rulers," *New York Times,* 4 July 1987, 4.

39. Susan Benesch, "Haiti: Gunmen Sought to Kill Press Freedom Along with Elections," *CPJ Update* (January–February 1988):1.

40. Merrill Collett, "Hazards Mount for Colombian Press," *CPJ Update* (January–February 1988):4.

41. Shirley Christian, "Chilean Editor and Two Others Are Found Slain," *New York Times,* 10 September 1986, 1.

CHAPTER 6

1. Michael Stohl, "Outside of a Small Circle of Friends: States, Genocide, Mass Killings and the Role of Bystanders," *Journal of Peace Research* 24(1987):154.

2. Alex P. Schmid and Janny de Graaf, *Violence as Communication: Insurgent Terrorism and the Western News Media* (Beverly Hills, Calif.: Sage Publications, 1982), 85.

3. Frederick Schiff, "Rewriting State-Sponsored Terrorism: The 'Dirty War' Reinterpreted by the Press in Argentina during the Period of Democratic Transition" (Paper presented to the Communication in Terrorist Events Conference, Boston, 3–5 March 1988).

4. Michael J. Kelly and Thomas H. Mitchell, "Transnational Terrorism and the Western Elite Press," *Political Communication and Persuasion* 1(1981):269–96.

5. Zoe Che-wei Tan, "Media Publicity and Insurgent Terrorism: A Twenty-Year Balance Sheet" (Paper presented to the International Communication Association Convention, Montreal, 25 May 1987).

6. Ronald D. Crelinsten, "Images of Terrorism in the Media, 1966–1985" (Paper presented to the Communication in Terrorist Events Conference, Boston, 3–5 March 1988).

7. Ronald D. Crelinsten, "Images of Terrorism in the Media, 1966–1985."

8. David L. Paletz et al., "Terrorism on TV News: The IRA, the FALN, and the Red Brigades," in *Television Coverage of International Affairs,* ed. William C. Adams (Norwood, N.J.: Ablex Publishing, 1985), 143–65.

9. David Altheide, "Three-in-One News: Network Coverage of Iran," *Journalism Quarterly* 59(Autumn 1982):482–86; and David Altheide, "Impact of Format and Ideology on TV News Coverage of Iran," *Journalism Quarterly* 62(Summer 1985):346–51.

10. Tony Atwater, "Network Evening News Coverage of the TWA Hostage Crisis," *Journalism Quarterly* 64(Summer–Autumn 1987):520–25.

11. Robert G. Picard, "Stages in Coverage of Incidents of Political Violence," *Terrorism and the News Media Research Project Monograph Series* (Boston: Emerson College, 1988).

12. Paletz et al., "Terrorism on TV News."

13. David L. Paletz et al., "The I.R.A., the Red Brigades, and the F.A.L.N. in the *New York Times*," *Journal of Communication* 32(Spring 1982):162–72.

14. Warren Decker and Daniel Rainey, "Media and Terrorism: Toward the Development of an Instrument to Explicate Their Relationship" (Paper presented to the annual meeting of the Speech Communication Association, Louisville, Kentucky, 4–7 November 1982).

15. Atwater, "Network Evening News Coverage of the TWA Hostage Crisis."

16. Picard, "Stages in Coverage of Incidents of Political Violence."

17. Jerry Levin, "Remarks to Committee to Protect Journalists," *Political Communication and Persuasion* 4(1987):25.

18. L. John Martin and Yossi Draznin, "Broadcast Gatekeepers' Views on Media Coverage of Terrorism" (Paper presented to the Communication in Terrorist Events Conference, Boston, 3–5 March 1988).

19. Michael A. Milburn et al., "An Attributional Analysis of the Mass Media Coverage of Terrorism" (Paper presented to the annual meeting of the International Society for Political Psychology, San Francisco, July 1987).

20. Linda K. Fuller, "Terrorism As Treated by the *Christian Science Monitor,* 1977–1987" (Paper presented to the Communication in Terrorist Events Conference, Boston, 3–5 March 1988).

21. Altheide, "Three-in-One News."

22. Atwater, "Network Evening News Coverage of the TWA Hostage Crisis."

23. Altheide, "Three-in-One News," 482.

24. Warren Decker and Daniel Rainey, "Media and Terrorism: Toward the Development of an Instrument to Explicate Their Relationship" (Paper presented to the Speech Communication Association annual meeting, Louisville, Kentucky, 4–7 November 1982).

25. Milan D. Meeske and Mohammed H. Javaheri, "Network Television Coverage of the Iranian Hostage Crisis," *Journalism Quarterly* 59(Winter 1982):643.

26. Robert G. Picard and Paul D. Adams, "Characterizations of Acts and Perpetrators of Political Violence in Three Elite U.S. Daily Newspapers," *Political Communication and Persuasion* 4(1987):1–9.

27. Decker and Rainey, "Media and Terrorism."

28. Atwater, "Network Evening News Coverage of the TWA Hostage Crisis."

29. Altheide, "Three-in-One News."

30. James F. Larson, "Television and U.S. Foreign Policy: The Case of the Iran Hostage Crisis," *Journal of Communication* 36(1986):108–27.

31. Paletz et al., "Terrorism on TV News," 162.

32. Sandra Wurth-Hough, "Network News Coverage of Terrorism: The Early Years," *Terrorism* 6(1983):418.

33. Paul D. Adams, "Newspaper Headline Words on Stories about Terrorism" (Paper presented to the Western Communication Educators Conference, Fresno, California, 14 November 1987).

34. L. John Martin, "The Media's Role in International Terrorism" (Paper presented to the Association for Education in Journalism and Mass Communication Convention, Corvallis, Oregon, 1983).

35. Paletz et al., "Terrorism on TV News."

36. Herbert A. Terry, "Television and Terrorism: Professionalism Not Quite the Answer," *Indiana Law Review* 53(1978):754.

37. Atwater, "Network Evening News Coverage of the TWA Hostage Crisis," 525.

38. Doris A. Graber, "Evaluating Crime-Fighting Policies: Media Images and Public Perspective," in *Evaluating Alternative Law-Enforcement Policies,* ed. Ralph Baker and Fred Meyer, Jr. (Lexington, Mass.: D. C. Heath, 1979), 179–99.

39. Michael B. Salwen and Jung-Sook Lee, "News of Terrorism: A Comparison of U.S. and South Korean Press," *Terrorism* 11(1988):323–28.

40. Mario Morcellini, "L'Informazione Periodica in Televisione" and "L'Attualita' Televisiva: Struttura Dell'Offerta Informativa Sul Territorio," in RAI Radiotelevisione Italiana, *Terrorismo e TV,* Vol. 1 (Rome: RAI, 1982).

41. George H. Quester, "Cruise-Ship Terrorism and the Media," *Political Communication and Persuasion* 3(1986):355–70.

42. Phillip Kurz, "Terrorism and TV: When the Challenge Comes, Will You Be Ready?" *Television Broadcast* (July 1986):44.

43. Paul Watzlawick, *How Real Is Real?* (New York: Random House, 1976), xi.

44. Thomas C. Cooper, "Terrorism and Perspectivist Philosophy: Understanding Adversarial News Coverage," *Terrorism and the News Media Research Project Monograph Series* (Boston: Emerson College, 1988).

45. Michael A. Milburn et al., "An Attributional Analysis of the Mass Media Coverage of Terrorism."

46. Michael A. Milburn et al., "Survey and Experimental Studies of the Effect of Television News on Individuals' Attributions about Terrorism" (Paper presented to the annual meeting of the International Society for Political Psychology, Meadowlands, New Jersey, 4 July 1988).

47. Patrick Clawson, "Why We Need More but Better Coverage of Terrorism," *Orbis* (Winter 1987):704.

48. David L. Altheide, "Format and Symbols in TV Coverage of Terrorism in the United States and Great Britain" (Paper presented to the Pacific Sociological Association, Denver, 9–12 April 1986).

49. Edward C. Epstein, "The Uses of 'Terrorism': A Study in Media Bias," *Stanford Journal of International Studies* 12(Spring 1977):67.

50. Ozyegin, Nejat, "Construction of the 'Facts' of Political Violence: A Content Analysis of Press Coverage," (M.A. thesis, University of Pennsylvania, 1986).

51. Thomas C. Cooper, "Terrorism and Perspectivist Philosophy."

52. David Rubin and Lyn Fine, "The Soviet Union as State Terrorist: *Time* Magazine Coverage of Soviet Military Activity in Afghanistan" (Paper presented to the Communication in Terrorist Events Conference, Boston, 3–5 March 1988).

53. Ronald D. Crelinsten, "Images of Terrorism in the Media, 1966–1985."

54. Picard and Adams, "Characterizations of Acts and Perpetrators of Political Violence in Three Elite U.S. Daily Newspapers."

55. Judith Buddenbaum, "Of Christian Freedom Fighters and Marxist Terrorists: Images of SWAPO and the Namibian Independence Movement in the Religious and Secular Press" (Paper presented to the Communication in Terrorist Events Conference, Boston, 3–5 March 1988).

56. Philip Schlesinger et al., *Televising 'Terrorism': Political Violence in Popular Culture* (London: Comedia, 1983).

57. Fred W. Friendly, "International Terrorism and Journalism" (Remarks to the Association of Schools of Journalism and Mass Communication, Memphis, Tennessee, 4 August 1986).

58. James F. Larson, "Television and U.S. Foreign Policy: The Case of the Iran Hostage Crisis," *Journal of Communication* 36(Autumn 1986):108–27.

59. Quoted in Francis Dale, "One Man's Freedom Fighter Is Another Man's Terrorist," *World Media Report* (1987):147.

60. Patricia R. Palmerton, "Terrorism and Institutional Targets As Portrayed by News Providers" (Paper presented to the Speech Communication Association, Denver, Colorado, 1985).

61. David L. Altheide, "Iran vs. U.S. TV News: The Hostage Story Out of Context," in *Television Coverage of the Middle East,* ed. William C. Adams (Norwood, N.J.: Ablex Publishing, 1981), 128–58.

62. Patricia R. Palmerton, "The Rhetoric of Terrorism and the Media Response to the 'Crisis in Iran,'" *Western Journal of Speech Communication* 52(Spring 1988):105–21.

63. Gerard A. Hauser, "Setting Foreign Policy in the Public Sphere: Carter on the Iranian Hostages" (Paper presented to the Speech Communication Association, Louisville, Kentucky, November 1982).

64. Ralph E. Dowling, "Rhetorical Vision and Print Journalism: Reporting the Iran Hostage Crisis to America" (Ph.D. diss., University of Denver, 1984).

65. See Jack Lule, "Sacrifice, Scapegoat, and the Body on the Tarmac: A Terrorist Victim in the *New York Times*" (Paper presented to the Communication in Terrorist Events Conference, Boston, 3–5 March 1988); and Jack Lule, "The Myth of My Widow: A Dramatistic Analysis of News Portrayals of a Terrorist Victim," *Terrorism and the News Media Research Project Monograph Series* (Boston: Emerson College, 1988).

CHAPTER 7

1. Bertrand Russell has observed that "an individual may be influenced: *a*. By direct physical power over his body, e.g. when he is imprisoned or killed; *b*. By rewards and punishments as inducements, e.g. in giving or withholding employment; *c*. By influence on opinion, i.e. propaganda in its broadest sense." See Bertrand Russell, *Power* (New York: W. W. Norton, 1969), 36.

2. Daniel J. Boorstin, *The Image: Or What Happened to the American Dream* (New York: Atheneum, 1961).

3. Philip Schlesinger et al., *Televising "Terrorism": Political Violence in Popular Culture* (London: Comedia, 1983), 136.

4. Patty Millett, "Pruning Back the Branches: Legislating Virtue in the News Media's Coverage of Terrorism" (Unpublished paper, Department of Justice, Harvard University Law School, 1988), 73–74.

5. George Gerbner, "Symbolic Functions of Violence and Terror," *Terrorism and the News Media Research Project Monograph Series* (Boston: Emerson College, 1988).

6. Gabriel Weimann, "Conceptualizing the Effects of Mass-Mediated Terrorism," *Political Communication and Persuasion* 4(1987):214.

7. Patrick Clawson, "Why We Need More but Better Coverage of Terrorism," *Orbis* (Winter 1987):701–2.

8. David L. Paletz et al., "Terrorism on TV News: The IRA, the FALN, and the Red Brigades." In *Coverage of International Affairs,* ed. William C. Adams (Norwood, N.J.: Ablex Publishing, 1982).

9. These determinants of salience apply not only to adults but are found even among children who receive information from the media. A study of children's knowledge about the conflict in Northern Ireland found that the knowledge of children in Northern Ireland and Ireland was influenced by both proximity to the violence and higher television viewer-

ship. See Ed Cairns, "The Television News as a Source for Knowledge about the Violence for Children in Ireland: The Knowledge-Gap of Hypothesis," *Current Psychological Research and Reviews* 3(Winter 1984):32–38.

10. See, for example, Jennings Bryant et al., "Television Viewing and Anxiety," *Journal of Communication* 31(1981):106–19; Dolf Zillman and Jacob Wakshlag, "Fear of Victimization and the Appeal of Crime Drama," in *Selective Exposure to Communication,* ed. Dolf Azillman and Jennings Bryant (Hillsdale, N.J.: Lawrence Erlbaum, 1985); Doris Graber, "Evaluating Crime-Fighting Policies: Media Images and Public Perspective," in *Evaluating Alternative Law-Enforcement Policies,* ed. Ralph Baker and Fred Meyer, Jr. (Lexington, Mass.: D. C. Heath, 1979), 179–99; and Barrie Gunter and Mallory Wober, "Television Viewing and Public Perceptions of Hazards to Life," *Journal of Environmental Psychology* 3(1983):325–35.

11. Anthony Doob and Glenn Macdonald, "The News Media and Perceptions of Violence," in *Report of the Royal Commission on Violence in the Communications Industry,* Vol. 5, *Learning from the Media* (Toronto: Royal Commission on Violence in the Communications Industry, 1977), 171–226.

12. Yonah Alexander, "Terrorism, the Media and the Police," *Journal of International Affairs* 32(1978):112.

13. Katharine Graham, "Terrorism and the Media" (Speech to the American Newspaper Publishers Association Government Affairs Dinner, Washington, D.C., 6 March 1986).

14. J. Bowyer Bell, *Transnational Terror* (Washington, D.C.: American Enterprise Institute, 1975), 89.

15. Abraham H. Miller, *Terrorism, the Media and the Law* (Dobbs Ferry, N.Y.: Transnational, 1982), 24.

16. National Advisory Committee on Criminal Justice Standards and Goals, *Disorders and Terrorism: Report of the Task Force on Disorders and Terrorism* (Washington, D.C.: Law Enforcement Assistance Administration, 1977), 65.

17. Ibid., 368.

18. Jeffery Z. Rubin and Nehemia Friedland, "Theater of Terror," *Psychology Today,* March 1986, 28.

19. Ralph E. Dowling, "Terrorism and the Media: A Rhetorical Genre," *Journal of Communication* 36(Winter 1986):12–24.

20. Lowndes F. Stephens, "How Should We Evaluate Press Coverage of Terrorism?" (Paper presented to the Communication in Terrorist Events Conference, Boston, 3–5 March 1988).

Bibliography

BOOKS

Adams, William C., ed. *Television Coverage of International Affairs.* Norwood, N.J.: Ablex Publishing, 1982.
———. *Television Coverage of the Middle East.* Norwood, N.J.: Ablex Publishing, 1981.
Alali, A. Odasuo, and Kenoye Kelvin Eke, eds. *Media Coverage of Terrorism: Methods of Diffusion.* Newbury Park, Calif.: Sage, 1991.
Alexander, Yonah, and John M. Gleason, eds. *Behavioral and Quantitative Perspectives on Terrorism.* New York: Pergamon Press, 1981.
Alexander, Yonah, and S. M. Finger, eds. *Terrorism: Interdisciplinary Perspectives.* New York: John Jay Press, 1977.
Alexander, Yonah, and Robert G. Picard, eds. *In the Camera's Eye: News Coverage of Terrorist Events.* Washington, D.C.: Brassey's, 1991.
Alexander, Yonah, David Carlton, and Paul Wilkinson, eds. *Terrorism: Theory and Practice.* Boulder, Colo.: Westview Press, 1979.
Alexander, Yonah, Marjorie Browne, and Allen Nanes, eds. *Control of Terrorism.* New York: Crane, Rusak, 1979.
Altschull, J. Herbert. *Agents of Power: The Role of the News Media in Human Affairs.* New York: Longman, 1984.
Baradat, Leon P. *Political Ideologies: Their Origins and Impact.* Englewood Cliffs, N.J.: Prentice-Hall, 1979.
Barry, Brian. *Sociologists, Economics and Democracy.* London: Collier-Macmillan, 1970.
Bassiouni, M. Cherif, ed. *International Terrorism and Political Crimes.* Springfield, Ill.: Charles C. Thomas, 1975.
Bell, J. Bowyer. *Transnational Terror.* Washington, D.C.: American Enterprise Institute, 1975.
Berlo, David. *The Process of Communication.* New York: Holt, Rinehart, and Winston, 1960.

Boorstin, Daniel J. *The Image: Or What Happened to the American Dream.* New York: Atheneum, 1961.

Cantril, Hadley. *Gauging Public Opinion.* Princeton, N.J.: Princeton University Press, 1947.

Clutterbuck, Richard. *The Media and Political Violence.* 2d ed. London: Macmillan, 1983.

Committee to Protect Journalists. *Attacks on the Press 1987.* New York: Committee to Protect Journalists, 1988.

Ellul, Jacques. *Propaganda.* New York: Alfred Knopf, 1965.

European Terrorism and the Media. London: International Press Institute, 1978.

Freedman, Lawrence Z., and Yonah Alexander, eds. *Perspectives on Terrorism.* Wilmington, Del.: Scholarly Resources, 1983.

Friedlander, R. A. *Terrorism and the Media: A Contemporary Assessment.* Gaithersburg, Md.: International Association of Chiefs of Police, 1981.

Gurr, Ted Robert. *Why Men Rebel.* Princeton, N.J.: Princeton University Press, 1971.

Hachten, William. *The World News Prism: Changing Media, Clashing Ideologies.* Ames: Iowa State University Press, 1981.

Hall, Stuart, C. Critcher, T. Jeggerson, J. Clarke, and B. Roberts. *Policing the Crisis: Mugging, the State and Law and Order.* London: Macmillan, 1978.

Herman, Edward S. *The Real Terror Network: Terrorism in Fact and Propaganda.* Boston: South End Press, 1982.

Karlins, Marvin, and Herbert Abelson. *Persuasion: How Opinions and Attitudes Are Changed.* 2d ed. New York: Springer Publishing, 1970.

Katz, Elihu, and Paul Lazarsfeld. *Personal Influence.* Glencoe, Ill.: Free Press, 1954.

Khaldun, Ibn. Translated by Franz Rosenthal and edited by N. J. Dawood. *The Muqaddimah: An Introduction to History.* Princeton, N.J.: Princeton University Press, 1967.

Lasswell, Harold D. *Propaganda Techniques in the World War.* New York: Alfred Knopf, 1927.

Livingstone, Neil C. *The War against Terrorism.* Lexington, Mass.: Lexington Books, 1982.

Lovell, Ronald P. *Inside Public Relations.* Boston: Allyn and Bacon, 1982.

Maslow, Abraham. *Motivation and Personality.* New York: Harper and Row, 1970.

Merton, Robert. *Social Theory and Social Structure.* Glencoe, Ill.: Free Press, 1949.

Midgley, Sarah, and Virginia Rice, eds. *Terrorism and the Media in the 1980s.* Washington, D.C.: The Media Institute, 1984.

Miller, Abraham, ed. *Terrorism, the Media and the Law.* Dobbs Ferry, N.Y.: Transnational, 1982.

National Advisory Committee on Criminal Justice Standards and Goals. *Disorders and Terrorism: Report of the Task Force on Disorders and Terrorism.* Washington, D.C.: Law Enforcement Assistance Administration, 1977.

O'Neill, Michael J. *Terrorist Spectaculars: Should TV Coverage Be Curbed?* New York: Priority Press, 1986.

Picard, Robert G. *The Press and the Decline of Democracy.* Westport, Conn.: Greenwood Press, 1985.

Picard, Robert G., and Rhonda S. Sheets. *Terrorism and the News Media Research Bibliography.* Columbia, S.C.: Association for Education in Journalism and Mass Communication, 1986.

Rank, Hugh. *The Pep Talk: How to Analyze Political Language.* Park Forest, Ill.: Counter-Propaganda Press, 1984.

Roucek, Joseph S., ed. *Social Control for the 1980s: A Handbook for Order in a Democratic Society.* Westport, Conn.: Greenwood Press, 1978.

Russell, Bertrand. *Power.* New York: W. W. Norton, 1969.

Schlesinger, Philip, Graham Murdock, and Philip Elliott. *Televising 'Terrorism': Political Violence in Popular Culture.* London: Comedia, 1983.

Schmid, Alex Peter. *Political Terrorism: A Research Guide to Concepts, Theories, Data Bases and Literature.* New Brunswick, N.J.: Transaction Books, 1984.

Schmid, Alex P., and Janny de Graff. *Insurgent Terrorism and the Western News Media: An Exploratory Analysis with a Dutch Case Study.* Leiden: Dutch State University, 1980.

_____. *Violence as Communication: Insurgent Terrorism and the Western News Media.* Beverly Hills, Calif.: Sage Publications, 1982.

Schramm, Wilbur, and Doris Roberts, eds. *The Process and Effects of Mass Communication.* Urbana: University of Illinois Press, 1971.

Siebert, Fred S., Theodore Peterson, and Wilbur Schramm. *Four Theories of the Press.* Urbana: University of Illinois Press, 1956.

Snyder, Marie, ed. *Media and Terrorism: The Psychological Impact.* North Newton, Kans.: Mennonite Press, 1978.

Spencer, Herbert. *Principles of Sociology.* Edited by Stanislav Andreski. London: Macmillan, 1969.

Stohl, Michael, ed. *The Politics of Terrorism.* 3d ed. New York: Marcel Dekker, 1988.

Stohl, Michael, and George A. Lopez, eds. *The State as Terrorist: The Dynamics of Governmental Violence and Repression.* Westport, Conn.: Greenwood Press, 1984.

Television and Conflict. London: Institute for the Study of Conflict, 1978.

Terrorism and the Media. London: International Press Institute, 1980.

Terrorism and the Media. Washington, D.C.: American Legal Foundation, 1986.

Watzlawick, Paul. *How Real Is Real?* New York: Random House, 1976.

ARTICLES, BOOK CHAPTERS, MONOGRAPHS

Alexander, Yonah. "Communications Aspects of International Terrorism." *International Problems* 16(1977):55–60.

_____. "Terrorism and the Media: Some Observations." *Terrorism* 3:(1980)179–80.

_____. "Terrorism, the Media and the Police." *Journal of International Affairs* 32(1978):101–13.

Altheide, David. "Impact of Format and Ideology on TV News Coverage of Iran." *Journalism Quarterly* 62(Summer 1985):346–51.

_____. "Network News: Oversimplified and Underexplained." *Washington Journalism Review* (May 1981):28–29.

_____. "Three-In-One News: Network Coverage of Iran." *Journalism Quarterly* 59(Autumn 1982):482–86.

Anable, David. "Media, Reluctant Participant in Terrorism." In *Media and Terrorism: The Psychological Impact,* edited by Marie Snyder, 15–22. North Newton, Kans.: Mennonite Press, 1978.

Atwater, Tony. "Network Evening News Coverage of the TWA Hostage Crisis." *Journalism Quarterly* 64(Summer–Autumn 1987):520–25.

Baker, Brent. "The PAO and Terrorism." *Military Media Review* (July 1986):10–11.

Bassiouni, M. Cherif. "Media Coverage of Terrorism: The Law and the Public." *Journal of Communication* 32(Spring 1982):128–43.

_____. "Problems in Media Coverage of Nonstate-Sponsored Terror-Violence Incidents." In *Perspectives on Terrorism,* edited by Lawrence Z. Freedman and Yonah Alexander, 177–200. Wilmington, Del.: Scholarly Resources, 1983.

_____. "Terrorism, Law Enforcement and the Mass Media." *Journal of Criminal Law and Criminology* 72(1981):801–51.

Bell, J. B. "Terrorist Scripts and Live-Action Spectaculars." *Columbia Journalism Review* (May 1978): 47–50.

Bellman, Joel. "BBC: Clearing the Air." *The Journalist* 4(January 1986):20–23.

Bennett, James R. "Page One Sensationalism and the Libyan 'Hit Team.'" *Newspaper Research Journal* 4(Spring 1983):34–38.

Boyer, Peter J. "Arab's Interview Stirs News Debate." *New York Times,* 7 May 1986, A7.

Bryant, Jennings, Rodney Corveth, and Dan Brown. "Television Viewing and Anxiety." *Journal of Communication* 31(1981):106–19

Cairns, Ed. "The Television News as a Source for Knowledge about the Violence for Children in Ireland: A Test of the Knowledge-Gap Hypothesis." *Current Psychological Research and Reviews* 3(Winter 1984):32–38.

Catton, W. R., Jr. "Militants and the Media: Partners in Terrorism?" *Indiana Law Journal* 53(1978):703–15.

Clawson, Patrick. "Why We Need More but Better Coverage of Terrorism." *Orbis* 30(Winter 1987):701–10.

Collins, R. "Terrorism and the Mass Media." *Intermedia* 10(January 1982):48–50.

"Conference Report: Terrorism and the Media," *Political Communication and Persuasion* 3(1985):185–90.

Consoli, John. "Covering Terrorism." *Editor and Publisher* (November 2, 1985):11.

Cooper, Thomas. "Terrorism and Perspectivist Philosophy: Understanding Adversarial News Coverage." *Terrorism and the News Media Research Project Monograph Series.* Boston: Emerson College, 1988.

Cox, Robert. "The Media as a Weapon." *Political Communication and Persuasion* 1(1981):297–300.

Crelinsten, Ronald. "Power and Meaning: Terrorism as a Struggle over Access to the Communication Structure." In *Contemporary Research on Terrorism,* edited by Paul Wilkinson. Aberdeen, Scotland: University of Aberdeen Press, 1987.

Crenshaw, Martha. "The Causes of Terrorism." *Comparative Politics* 13(July 1981):379–99.

Dale, Francis. "One Man's Freedom Fighter Is Another Man's Terrorist." *World Media Report* 1(1987):139–48.

Doob, Anthony, and Glenn Macdonald. "The News Media and Perceptions of Violence." In *Report of the Royal Commission on Violence in the Communications Industry.* Vol. 5, *Learning from the Media,* 171–226. Toronto: Royal Commission on Violence in the Communications Industry, 1977.

Dowling, Ralph E. "Terrorism and the Media: A Rhetorical Genre." *Journal of Communication* 36(Winter 1986):12–24.

Elliot, Philip, Graham Murdock, and Philip Schlesinger. "Terrorism and the State: A Case Study of the Discourses of Television." *Media, Culture and Society* 5(April 1983):155–77.

Elliott, Deni. "Family Ties: A Case Study of Families and Friends During the Hijacking of TWA Flight 847." *Political Communication and Persuasion* 5(1988):67–75.

Epstein, E. C. "The Uses of 'Terrorism': A Study in Media Bias." *Stanford Journal of International Studies* 12(1977):67–78.

Friedland, Nehemia. "The Psychological Impact of Terrorism: A Double-Edged Sword." *Political Psychology* 6(December 1985):591–604.

Gerbner, George. "Symbolic Functions of Violence and Terror." *Terrorism and the News Media Research Project Monograph Series.* Boston: Emerson College, 1988.

Graber, Doris. "Evaluating Crime-Fighting Policies: Media Images and Public Perspective." In *Evaluating Alternative Law-Enforcement Policies,* edited by Ralph Baker and Fred Meyer, Jr., 179–99. Lexington, Mass.: D. C. Heath, 1979.

Grossman, Larry. "The Face of Terrorism." *The Quill* 74(June 1986):38.

Gunter, Barrie, and Mallory Wober. "Television Viewing and Public Perceptions of Hazards to Life." *Journal of Environmental Psychology* 3(1983):325–35.

Heyman, Edward, and Edward Mickolus. "Observations on 'Why Violence Spreads.'" *International Studies Quarterly* 24(June 1980):299–305.

Hickey, Neil. "Terrorism and Television." *TV Guide,* 31 July 1976, 4.

Hill, Frederic B. "Media Diplomacy: Crisis Management with an Eye on the TV Screen." *Washington Journalism Review* 3(May 1981):23–27.

Jaehnig, Walter B. "Journalists and Terrorism: Captives of the Libertarian Tradition." *Indiana Law Journal* 53(Summer 1978):717–44.

Jenkins, Brian M. "The Psychological Implications of Media-Covered Terrorism." *Rand Paper Series* (1981).

Johnpoll, B. "Terrorism and the Mass Media in the United States." In *Terrorism:*

Interdisciplinary Perspectives, edited by Yonah Alexander and S. M. Finger. New York: John Jay Press, 1977.

Jones, Juanita B., and Abraham H. Miller. "The Media and Terrorist Activity: Resolving the First Amendment Dilemma." *Ohio Northern University Law Review* 6(1979):70–81.

Kaplan, Peter W. "Competition over Hostages Is Fierce for the U.S. Television Networks in Beirut." *New York Times,* 20 June 1985, A17.

Katz, Elihu. "Communications Research and the Image of Society: Convergence of Two Research Traditions." *American Journal of Sociology* 65(1960):435–40.

———. "The Two-Step Flow of Communication: An Up-to-Date Report on an Hypothesis." *Public Opinion Quarterly* 21(Spring 1957):61–78.

Kecskemeti, Paul. "Propaganda." In *Handbook of Communication,* edited by Ithiel de Sola Pool and Wilbur Schramm. Chicago: Rand McNally College Publishing, 1973.

Kelly, Michael J., and Thomas H. Mitchell. "Transnational Terrorism and the Western Elite Press." *Political Communication and Persuasion* 1(1981):269–96.

Kurz, Phillip. "Terrorism and TV." *Television Broadcast* (July 1986):44–48.

Larson, James F. "Television and U.S. Foreign Policy: The Case of the Iran Hostage Crisis." *Journal of Communication* 36(1986):108–27.

Levin, Jerry. "Remarks to Committee to Protect Journalists." *Political Communication and Persuasion* 4(1987):25–27.

Levy, Rudolf. "Terrorism and the Mass Media." *Military Intelligence* (October–December 1985):34–38.

Lule, Jack. "The Myth of My Widow: A Dramatistic Analysis of News Portrayals of a Terrorist Victim." *Terrorism and the News Media Research Project Monograph Series.* Boston: Emerson College, 1988.

McLeod, Jack, Lee Becker, and James Byrnes. "Another Look at the Agenda-Setting Function of the Press." *Communication Research* 1(April 1974):131–66.

Martin, L. John. "Mass Media Treatment of Terrorism." *Terrorism* 8(1985):127–46.

———. "Violence, Terrorism, Non-Violence: Vehicles of Social Control." In *Social Control for the 1980s: A Handbook for Order in a Democratic Society,* edited by Joseph Roucek, 183–93. Westport, Conn.: Greenwood Press, 1978.

Meeske, Milan D., and Mohamad Hamid Javaheri. "Network Television Coverage of the Iranian Hostage Crisis." *Journalism Quarterly* 59(Winter 1982):641–45.

Midlarsky, Manus I., Martha Crenshaw, and Fumihiko Yoshida. "Why Violence Spreads: The Contagion of International Terrorism." *International Studies Quarterly* 24(June 1980):262–98.

Miller, Abraham H. "Terrorism and the Media: A Dilemma." *Terrorism* 3(1979):79–89.

Morcellini, Mario. "L'Informazione Periodica in Televisione," and "L'Attualita

Televisiva: Struttura Dell'Offerta Informativa Sul Territorio." In *Terrorismo e TV,* Vol. 1. Rome: RAI Radiotelevisione Italiana, 1982.

O'Donnell, Wendy M. "Prime Time Hostages: A Case Study of Coverage of the Hijacking and Hostage-Taking on TWA Flight 847." *Terrorism and the News Media Research Project Monograph Series.* Boston: Emerson College, 1988.

Paletz, David L., John Z. Ayanian, and Peter A. Fozzard. "The I.R.A., the Red Brigades, and the F.A.L.N. in the *New York Times." Journal of Communication* 32(Spring 1982):162-72.

————. "Terrorism on TV News: The IRA, the FALN, and the Red Brigades." In *Television Coverage of International Affairs,* edited by William C. Adams, 143-65. Norwood, N.J.: Ablex Publishing, 1982.

Palmerton, Patricia R. "The Rhetoric of Terrorism and the Media Response to the 'Crisis in Iran.' " *Western Journal of Speech Communication* 52(Spring 1988):105-21.

Picard, Robert G. "The Conundrum of News Coverage of Terrorism." *Toledo Law Review* 18(Fall 1986):141-50.

————. "News Coverage as the Contagion of Terrorism: Dangerous Charges Backed by Dubious Science." *Political Communication and Persuasion* 3(1986):385-400.

————. "Stages in Coverage of Incidents of Political Violence." *Terrorism and the News Media Research Project Monograph Series.* Boston: Emerson College, 1988.

————. "Words on War and Conflict." *St. Louis Journalism Review* 13(September 1983):21-22.

Picard, Robert G., and Paul D. Adams. "Characterizations of Acts and Perpetrators of Terrorism in Three Elite U.S. Daily Newspapers." *Political Communication and Persuasion* 4(1987):1-9.

Post, Jerrold M. "Hostile, Conformite, Fraternite: The Group Dynamics of Terrorist Behavior." *International Journal of Group Psychotherapy* 36(April 1986):211-24.

Quester, George H. "Cruise Ship Terrorism and the Media." *Political Communication and Persuasion* 4(1986):355-70.

Rada, S. E. "Transnational Terrorism as Public Relations?" *Public Relations Review* 11(Fall 1985):26-33.

Rubin, Jeffrey, and Nehemia Friedland. "Theater of Terror." *Psychology Today,* March 1986, 21-28.

Salomone, Franco. "Terrorism and the Mass Media." In *International Terrorism and Political Crimes,* edited by M. Cherif Bassiouni, 43-47. Springfield, Ill.: Charles C. Thomas, 1975.

Salwen, Michael, and Jung-Sook Lee. "News of Terrorism: A Comparison of the U.S. and South Korean Press." *Terrorism* 11(1988):323-28.

Stephens, Lowndes F. "Implications of Terrorism for Planning the Public Relations Function." *Terrorism and the News Media Research Project Monograph Series.* Boston: Emerson College, 1988.

Stohl, Michael. "Outside of a Small Circle of Friends: States, Genocide, Mass

Killings and the Role of Bystanders." *Journal of Peace Research* 24(1987):151–66.

Terry, H. A. "Television and Terrorism: Professionalism Not Quite the Answer." *Indiana Law Journal* 53(1978):745–77.

Weimann, Gabriel. "Conceptualizing the Effects of Mass-Mediated Terrorism." *Political Communication and Persuasion* 4(1987):213–16.

_____. "Terrorists or Freedom Fighters? Labeling Terrorism in the Israeli Press." *Political Communication and Persuasion* 2(1985):433–45.

_____. "The Theater of Terror: Effects of Press Coverage." *Journal of Communication* 33(Winter 1985):38–45.

Wurth-Hough, Sandra. "Network News Coverage of Terrorism: The Early Years." *Terrorism* 6(1983):403–22.

Zillman, Dolf, and Jacob Wakshlag. "Fear of Victimization and the Appeal of Crime Drama." In *Selective Exposure to Communication,* edited by Dolf Zillman and Jennings Bryant. Hillsdale, N.J.: Lawrence Erlbaum, 1985.

UNPUBLISHED MATERIALS

Adams, Paul D. "Newspaper Headline Words on Stories about Terrorism." Paper presented to the Western Communication Educators Conference, Fresno, California, November 14, 1987.

Altheide, David L. "Format and Symbols in TV Coverage of Terrorism in the United States and Great Britain." Paper presented to the Pacific Sociological Association Convention, Denver, April 9–12, 1986.

Buddenbaum, Judith. "Of Christian Freedom Fighters and Marxist Terrorists: Images of SWAPO and the Namibian Independence Movement in the Religious and Secular Press." Paper presented to the Communication in Terrorist Events Conference, Boston, March 3–5, 1988.

Crelinsten, Ronald D. "Images of Terrorism in the Media, 1966–1985." Paper presented to the Communication in Terrorist Events Conference, Boston, March 3–5, 1988.

Decker, Warren, and Daniel Rainey. "Media and Terrorism: Toward the Development of an Instrument to Explicate Their Relationship." Paper presented to the Speech Communication Association annual conference, Louisville, Kentucky, November 4–7, 1982.

Dowling, Ralph E. "Rhetorical Vision and Print Journalism: Reporting the Iran Hostage Crisis to America." Ph.D. diss., University of Denver, 1984.

_____. "The Terrorist and the Media: Partners in Crime or Rituals and Harmless Observers?" Paper presented to the "Media and Modern Warfare" conference, Centre for Conflict Studies, University of New Brunswick, Fredericton, New Brunswick, September 29–October 1, 1988.

Fine, Lyn, and David M. Rubin. "The Soviet Union as State Terrorist: *Time* Magazine Coverage of Soviet Military Activity in Afghanistan." Paper presented to the Communication in Terrorist Events Conference, Boston, March 3–5, 1988.

Flemming, Peter A., and Michael Stohl. "State Terrorism and the News Media." Paper presented to the Communication in Terrorist Events Conference, Boston, March 3–5, 1988.

Friendly, Fred W. "International Terrorism and Journalism." Remarks to the Association of Schools of Journalism and Mass Communication, Memphis, Tennessee, August 4, 1985.

Fuller, Linda K. "Terrorism As Treated by the *Christian Science Monitor,* 1976–1986." Paper presented to the Communication in Terrorist Events Conference, Boston, March 3–5, 1988.

Gallimore, Timothy. "Media Compliance with Voluntary Press Guidelines for Covering Terrorism." Paper presented to the Communication in Terrorist Events Conference, Boston, March 3–5, 1988.

Graham, Katharine. "Terrorism and the Media." Speech to the American Newspaper Publishers Association Government Affairs Dinner, Washington, D.C., March 6, 1986.

Hauser, Gerald A. "Setting Foreign Policy in the Public Sphere: Carter on the Iranian Hostages." Paper presented to the Speech Communication Association, Louisville, Kentucky, November 1982.

Holz, Josephine, Eric Cardinal, and Dennis Kerr. "The *Achille Lauro:* A Study in Terror." Paper presented to the American Association for Public Opinion Research, Hershey, Pennsylvania, May 14–17, 1987.

Lule, Jack. "Sacrifice, Scapegoat, and the Body on the Tarmac: A Terrorist Victim in the *New York Times.*" Paper presented to the Communication in Terrorist Events Conference, Boston, March 3–5, 1988.

Martin, L. John. "The Media's Role in International Terrorism." Paper presented to the Association for Education in Journalism and Mass Communication Annual Convention, Corvallis, Oregon, August 9, 1983.

Martin, L. John, and Yossi Draznin. "Broadcast Gatekeepers' Views on Media Coverage of Terrorism." Paper presented to the Communication in Terrorist Events Conference, Boston, March 3–5, 1988.

Milburn, Michael A., Brian Cistuli, and Marjorie Garr. "Survey and Experimental Studies of the Effect of Television News on Individuals' Attributions about Terrorism." Paper presented to the annual meeting of the International Society for Political Psychology, San Francisco, July 1987.

Milburn, Michael A., C. Bowley, J. Fay-Dumaine, and D. Kennedy. "An Attributional Analysis of the Mass Media Coverage of Terrorism." Paper presented to the annual meeting of the International Society for Political Psychology, Meadowlands, New Jersey, July 1988.

Millett, Patty. "Pruning Back the Branches: Legislating Virtue in the News Media's Coverage of Terrorism." Department of Justice, Harvard University Law School, 1988.

Nejat, Ozyegin. "Construction of the 'Facts' of Political Violence: A Content Analysis of Press Coverage." M.A. thesis, University of Pennsylvania, 1986.

Palmerton, Patricia. "Terrorism and Institutional Targets As Portrayed by News Providers." Paper presented to the Speech Communication Association Convention, Denver, Colorado, 1985.

Picard, Robert G. "Journalists as Targets and Victims of Terrorism." Paper presented to the Communication in Terrorist Events Conference, Boston, March 3–5, 1988.

Picard, Robert G. "The Socio-Institutional Context of Media in Terrorism." Paper presented to the "Media and Modern Warfare" conference, Centre for Conflict Studies, University of New Brunswick, Fredericton, New Brunswick, September 29–October 1, 1988.

Schiff, Frederick. "Rewriting State Sponsored Terrorism: The 'Dirty War' Reinterpreted by the Press in Argentina during the Period of Democratic Transition." Paper presented to the Communication in Terrorist Events Conference, Boston, March 3–5, 1988.

Stephens, Lowndes F. "How Should We Evaluate Press Performance in Covering Terrorism?" Paper presented to the Communication in Terrorist Events Conference, Boston, March 3–5, 1988.

Tan, Zoe Che-wei. "Media Publicity and Insurgent Terrorism: A Twenty-Five Year Balance Sheet." Paper presented to the International Communication Association Convention, Montreal, May 25, 1987.

Index